Best Copy Available

The following titles are bound-with items. Exact duplicates could not be found. Irregularities do exist.

BUFFALO BOARD OF TRADE.

ANNUAL STATEMENT

OF THE

TRADE AND COMMERCE

OF

BUFFALO FOR THE YEAR 1855,

TOGETHER WITH A REVIEW OF THE

GENERAL BUSINESS OF THE CITY.

BY JOHN J. HENDERSON,
SECRETARY OF THE BOARD OF TRADE.

BUFFALO:
MURRAY & BAKER, BOOK AND JOB PRINTERS, 200 MAIN STREET.

1856.

BUFFALO BOARD OF TRADE.

ANNUAL STATEMENT

OF THE

TRADE AND COMMERCE

OF

BUFFALO FOR THE YEAR 1855,

TOGETHER WITH A REVIEW OF THE

GENERAL BUSINESS OF THE CITY.

BY JOHN J. HENDERSON,
SECRETARY OF THE BOARD OF TRADE.

BUFFALO:
MURRAY & BAKER, BOOK AND JOB PRINTERS, 200 MAIN STREET.

1856.

BOARD OF TRADE ROOMS, MERCHANT'S EXCHANGE,
Buffalo, February 25th, 1856.

THE BOARD OF TRADE, OF BUFFALO:

Your Committee to whom was referred the matter of procuring for publication a Statement and Review of the [Trade] and Commerce of Buffalo for the year 1855, beg leave to submit for your consideration, the following Report, [prep]ared by JOHN J. HENDERSON, Secretary of your Board, who has devoted much time and attention to the com[pila]tion of the work, and your Committee take pleasure in recommending it, believing the same to be correct, and [emb]racing much valuable information and statistical facts, the importance of which are too well known and appre[ciat]ed by the public to require any extended notice at our hands. Very few persons are probably aware of the vast [amo]unt of labor required, and the numerous difficulties that arise, in procuring the necessary data for such a report, [and] when we take into consideration that the facts and figures are condensed, and the result only given, some faint [idea] of the labor performed may be gained by a perusal of this review.

[An] examination of this report suggests some facts to your Committee, the importance of which to the interests [of th]e State and business of Buffalo, may not be inappropriately alluded to in this connection. The business of the [past] season has been of a very gratifying character, and the various branches of our Commercial and Mechanical [inte]rests exhibit an unusual degree of prosperity, and show a very flattering increase over any previous year.— [Alth]ough we are all well aware, that Buffalo is the greatest grain depot, as well as greatest market in the world; [and] that she now stands as the first inland city in the country in point of commercial supremacy. We should not [cont]ent ourselves with these facts, or rely on our "natural position" for an increase of our trade. The enterprise, [pers]everance and capital of other places, less favorably located, are constantly being brought to bear against us, and [ever]y dollar's worth of property diverted from Buffalo, whether designed for Oswego, Ogdensburgh, Boston, New [Yor]k, Philadelphia or Baltimore, diverts business from the Erie Canal, and diminishes the revenue of the State.

[Th]e Erie Canal, under the fostering care of the State, has greatly facilitated the settlement of the Western States. [The] trade created thereby has increased from year to year, and has brought into existence and stimulated competing [rout]es. These routes are yearly diverting large quantities of produce which legitimately belong to the Canal.

[Th]e construction, during the past twenty-eight years, of a large number of railroads in the United States, has [effec]ted a great change in the carrying trade of our Canals. A very extended system of railroads has been adopted, [hav]ing since their introduction the completion of 23,242 miles, being an increase in the past four years of over [10,00]0 miles, a very large proportion of which has been built to transact the trade of the West, and a portion of it [come]s into direct competition with the Erie Canal. The capital and influence thus brought into existence have been [seve]rely felt in our Legislature in the restrictions and embarrassments that have been placed upon the completion of [the e]nlargement of the Canal by its being made the *pack-horse* to carry State debts foreign to its construction, there[by c]rippling its resources by increasing the rates of toll, and enabling railroad corporations to secure the carrying [trade] which legitimately belonged to it, and eventually compelling the State to resort to direct taxation to reim[burs]e the treasury.

[O]ur Committee would not urge any restrictions on railroads, believing that fair, open and unrestricted compe[titio]n will give a greater impetus to the carrying trade than any legislative enactments in the shape of tolls on these [line]s; and your Committee would strongly recommend, so far as may be practical, the removal of all restrictions on [our C]anals consistent with providing a sufficient revenue to defray the expenses of repairs and to secure the comple[tion] of the enlargement at an early day.

[Pa]st experience has shown that reduction of tolls have added to the tonnage and business of the Canals. And [we] believe that a still further reduction may be made with like success, entertaining as they do, the opinion that [the] reduction of tolls is due to the interests of the citizens of this State, and, moreover, that it is the imperative [duty] of the proper authorities to make such reduction.

[W]e have employed, on our State Canals, over 4000 boats, which are owned by forwarders and companies; a large [porti]on of which constitute the entire personal property of a large class of the citizens of our State, whose liveli[hood] is in a great measure dependent upon the patronage and business they receive during the season of Canal [navig]ation. The revenues from tolls are, to a certain extent, dependent upon the business of this class of our citi[zens.]

During the past two years the owners of Canal stock have been obliged to lay up a number of their boats for [sever]al months, not for the reason that the property was not in the country, but from the fact that a system of [prefe]rences existed in favor of competing routes, induced by the high rates of tolls on the Canal, thereby enabling [the] railroads to transport property as cheap, (having no tolls to pay,) depriving the State of the revenue, and a [worth]y class of citizens of business that would otherwise have inured to their benefit. The reduction of tolls would cheapen transportation in the same ratio; and property would be received from an extent of country f[ar] beyond the limits of our present supplies, thereby opening new territory and increasing our aggregate receipts- furnishing business for the Canal during the entire season, and adding wealth to our City.

Your Committee would strongly recommend that the tolls on flour, beef, butter, domestic spirits, wheat, rye and barley should be reduced to two mills per 1000 pounds per mile, and beef, tallow, hides, &c., to one and a ha[lf] mills per thousand pounds, and they contend that no good reason can be urged why the products of cattle should [be] charged with three mill tolls, (double that of the products of swine,) while the great bulk of the former finds its w[ay] to market by Rail Road, and the revenue therefrom lost to the State, while the larger proportion of the products [of] swine, finds its way to market via. the Canals. The facts are so striking that your Committee deem it only necessa[ry] to call your particular attention to the accompanying report to prove this assertion.

Your Committee would also invite your attention to the receipts and shipments of flour and grain. Also to t[he] difference between the shipments by Canal and Rail Road. A simple examination of the facts will show the impo[r]tance of this measure, and the necessity of action thereon.

It would not be well to close your examination with these few facts, but to ascertain what amount of the weste[rn] productions finds its way to the seaboard through Pennsylvania to Philadelphia and Baltimore, and by our Northe[rn] Rail Road routes for New York and Boston, as well as the Great Western and New York and Erie Roads, in ord[er] to form some idea of the enormous amount of property diverted from our Canals, which, if the facts could be giv[en] would show in the opinion of your committee that but a small proportion of the trade of our Canals now divert[ed] by the New York Central, and Buffalo and New York Rail Roads in comparison to the large quantities diverted [by] these powerful and rival routes.

In the above, we have not taken into consideration the immense traffic of the Ohio and Mississippi River via. N[ew] Orleans for New York. The only argument in favor of this route being the reduced rates of transportation nur[sed] and fostered in a great measure by our high rate of tolls upon our State Canals.

Let an influence be brought to bear to cheapen the rates of transportation, and foster this principle in our char[ge] upon property seeking this route, then "our natural position" would avail us something tangible, and tell upon [the] future prosperity of Buffalo, and ensure an early completion of the Canal enlargement, which will also tend to s[till] further cheapen transportation, and by the removal of Legislative enactments from our Canals and Rail Roads, leav[ing] the western products to seek the cheapest route to market, Buffalo will then have nothing to fear from all the ri[val] routes contemplated or in existence.

All of which is respectfully submitted,

J. S. BUELL,
S. H. FISH,
CYRUS CLARKE,
S. S. GUTHRIE.

Committee,

FOURTH ANNUAL STATEMENT

OF THE

TRADE AND COMMERCE OF BUFFALO

FOR THE YEAR 1855.

The year that has just closed has been a singularly prosperous one to our city, in every department of Trade, Commerce, and the mechanical pursuits generally. These interests were never in so healthy a condition, or less free from pecuniary embarrassment.

The West has never enjoyed so marked a degree of prosperity as during the year 1855, and never before have her boundless resources been in so rapid a process of development. While it is a source of gratification to us that our sister cities have progressed so rapidly in all the elements that go to make them great and prosperous, it is with a just pride that we observe the steady advancement our own favored city has made, and, while this is in the main owing to the obvious advantages of location which we enjoy, it is also attributable to the untiring energy and enterprise of our citizens in the endeavor to promote her interests and build up her reputation.

But few, even of our own citizens, are aware of the vast progress of our City in buildings and manufactures that has taken place within the past year. Houses have been erected in every part of the city in great numbers, and for actual inhabitants. Buildings have not been put up merely on speculation, but really to accommodate people who have been quietly flocking in upon us, called here by an increased and increasing business. The outlet of the immense Valley of the Lakes, of the vast prairies of the West, and of the Lake Superior country, must, as a matter of course, be a great city. Its growth will be certain and constant, and will keep pace with the growth of the country, for which it must ever be the depot for the reception of its surplus products, and the distributor of manufactures seeking a Western market.

When we sent everything to the West and brought nothing back, our growth was dependant upon a changing trade. But that change has gone by, and we now can calculate the increase of business both ways with great accuracy. The only element now wanting to ensure certain prosperity is the advancement of manufactures among us, and they are advancing with rapid strides, although much more may be done, and will be, when attention is called to the advantages afforded by our location. We have now numerous iron works, of various kinds, doing a thriving business, offering fair but not injurious competition, and giving plain proof that much more, even in that line, may be done here. Our Flouring Mills,

Tanneries, Woolen Factories, and other manufacturing establishments, are doing a flourishing business. We hold forth every inducement that can be asked; water power, population, and, above all, a market both from and to the West that will consume all we can make, and supply us with all we can demand.

The people of this country have not hitherto been aware of the inducements we can offer at this city for all kinds of manufactories. Indeed, our citizens themselves have scarcely been aware of them. This mist is now fast disappearing, and the brightning prospects only need be looked at to seem more glowing still. We ought to exert every nerve that we may keep pace with the requirements of the West; our capitalists and real estate owners ought to remember that every new manufactory adds greatly to the value of the real estate and business of the city, and that it is both their immediate and remote interest to invest their property in such manufactures as will not only return a fair per centage in immediate profit, but will add to the wealth of the city as a great whole. When people from abroad see that we here invest in the same way we recommend to them to invest, they will believe us, and require no further invitation, and each man who establishes himself here holds out inducements to his friends to do the same.

Census of Buffalo.

The Census taken during the early part of the past summer shows that no city in the State has grown so rapidly in the last five years as Buffalo. In 1810 she had a population of 1,508 persons. Towards the end of the year 1813, when it was a village of a few hundred houses, it was burnt to the ground by the English, but the little town soon rose from its ashes, and in the year 1820 numbered 2,095 persons. In 1830 it had a population of 8,668. The completion of the Erie Canal in 1825 had given a new impulse to the business of the place, and greatly accelerated the growth of its population. In 1835 it contained 15,661 souls, in 1840 18,213 persons, and in 1850 42,261, showing an increase of 113 per cent. from 1830 to 1840, and of 132 per cent. from 1840 to 1850. The population has increased most rapidly within the last five years, and numbers, according to the last census, 74,233. It is admitted on all hands, and we have every reason to suppose, that the census of the city has not been accurately taken. In every Ward there are families who were never called upon, and it is believed that our population exceeded 80,000 at the close of the year. But, with all the defects in the returns, the city presents a remarkable growth. An increase of *eighty* per cent. in five years ought to be considered satisfactory, especially when it is known that the prosperity of the city is of the most solid character. There is no city of its size and age in the country where so many men do business on their own capital, and in their own stores and warehouses, where the streets are so well paved, where the system of sewerage is so perfect, or where so large a portion of the inhabitants live in their own houses. Some Western towns may have outstripped it in a sort of mushroon growth, by the aid of foreign capital, but the progress of Buffalo is a healthy increase from its own resources. Situated at the foot of this great chain of inland seas, it must always command a large trade, while its vicinity to the coal mines of Pennsylvania gives it advantages for enlarging its already considerable manufactures.

The following is a transcript of the official census of the city:

Wards.	Total Population.	Entitled to Representation.	Native Voters.	Naturalized Voters.	Aliens.	People of Color not taxed.
1st	7,996	4,702	343	805	3,284	10
2d	5,897	4,413	892	248	1,468	16
3d	4,294	3,023	344	331	1,227	44
4th	8,000	5,042	408	726	2,722	236
5th	8,756	5,586	244	905	3,030	140
6th	7,354	3,747	49	643	3,475	132
7th	7,804	4,518	121	825	3,268	18
8th	5,407	3,078	226	327	1,399	7
9th	5,625	4,311	848	300	1,297	17
10th	5,238	3,852	512	317	1,378	8
11th	3,314	2,383	248	267	921	
12th	3,730	2,325	191	321	1,404	
13th	818	503	50	49	315	
Total	74,233	47,483	4,476	6,064	25,188	628

This sum total includes the population of the old town of Black Rock, which was two years ago annexed to the city.

The following table exhibits a comparative view of the increase of the population of both places, according to the census returns:

	Buffalo.	Black Rock.	Total.
1840	17,323	3,605	20,628
1845	29,773	3,833	33,656
1850	42,261	7,508	49,769
1855			74,223

A very large proportion of the population of Buffalo probably consists of persons of foreign birth and their children. The census will only give as foreigners those born out of the country, while their children are put down as natives. Unless we count the children of German and Irish parents as a part of the foreign population, the census will form no correct idea of its amount. The population of the Fifth, Sixth and Seventh Wards consists almost exclusively of Germans, and by far the greatest part of the inhabitants of the Fourth Ward are Germans also. These four wards which, taken together, (with the exception of a small part of the town of Black Rock) formed the old Fourth Ward, have, according to the last census returns, a population of 31,914 souls. If we offset the American population in these Wards against Germans in the nine other Wards, the result will be that the German population of Buffalo exceeds 30,000.

The population of Buffalo in 1850 was 42,261, and Black Rock, which is now included in our city, was 7,508, making a total of 49,769, and in 1855 it had increased to 74,223, showing an increase in five years of 24,464 persons, or about 80 per cent.

Our population within the city limits is sufficient for a Senatorial District, and entitles us to three Representatives in the Assembly. The question of the division of the County of Erie, and the erection of the City into a county by itself has been agitated for some time past. As a new apportionment will be made this year under the late census, it seems desirable that the proposed division of the county should at once be made to entitle us to the proper representation. The city now pays within a fraction of 73-100 of all the county expenses. This 73 per cent is represented in the Board of Supervisors by 13 members, and the remaining 27 per cent by 24. By the operation of the State School Law, the city pays to the county towns annually $8,200 to support the Common Schools.—The expenses of temporary relief to the poor is now sustained exclusively by the city. A new county will bring with it no new officers; in fact it can dispense with the Board of Supervisors. These, and other advantages which we might mention, seem to demand the erection of our city into a county by itself, and we trust that the suggestions of the Mayor in his Inaugural, in this respect will be carried out.

On the first of January, 1854, the City of Buffalo was enlarged by the annexation of a considerable territory, formerly within the limits of Black Rock. The number of acres admitted within the city limits was 23,710, while the old city extended over about 1800 acres. The assessors' valuation of real estate in the enlarged city was $20,063,045, of which Black Rock furnished $3,362,105. The valuation of this property, as equalized by a Committee of the Board of Supervisors, was set down at $24,681,497, of which Black Rock had $3,205,912. The value of the personal estate was estimated at $2,774,255, of which Black Rock had $75,000. The total amount of real and personal estate, as equalized, was fixed at $27,455,752, of which Black Rock was rated $3,281,512.

The Assessors, in revising the tables for 1856, exhibit the following statement, which shows a steady increase in the value of the real and personal estate of the city:

Valuation of the Taxable Property in the several Wards of the City of Buffalo for 1855:

No. of Ward.	Valuation of Real Estate.	Valuation of Personal Estate.	Total Valuation.
1st	$4,090,425	$1,348,522	$5,438,947
2d	3,200,140	1,020,128	4,220,268
3d	1,045,570	4,000	1,019,570
4th	1,999,160	108,700	2,107,860
5th	1,869,165	19,400	1,888,565
6th	829,285	3,000	832,285
7th	1,433,694	36,400	1,470,094
8th	3,431,145	1,151,542	4,582,687
9th	3,598,190	1,167,600	4,765,790
10th	2,462,595	313,050	2,775,645
11th	1,713,535	484,650	2,198,185
12th	1,108,810	54,800	1,163,610
13th	542,205	2,000	544,205
1855	$27,323,919	$5,713,792	$33,037,711
1854	25,949,391	4,024,118	29,973,509
1853	20,063,045	2,774,255	22,837,300
Inc. 1855	$1,374,528	$1,689,674	$3,064,202

Total Tax in Old Territory,......$242,700
  "   "   in New   "   30,880

Total Tax......$273,580

Per centage in Old Territory,......8 18-100 mills per cent.
   "   "   in New   "   ......4 42-100 "   "   "

These statements which are official, having been taken from the records in the departments of the city government, exhibit a gratifying increase in the prosperity of our city. From the Mayor's message we learn that that portion of the city debt which became due during the year 1855, with all interest which has accrued has been paid, and the means prepared to meet that which will become due during the next six months. The amount of the funded debt unpaid on the first Monday of January, 1856, was $466.000. The liabilities for the Fire and School Departments and on bonds issued for the purchase of Market Grounds, and Pest House Lot, amount to $109,063; making the entire debt of the city, chargeable upon the General Fund, $575,063. Of this sum, $425,063 is chargeable upon the territory included within the old city bounds exclusively. The balance being $150,000, are the bonds issued to the Buffalo and Brantford Railroad Company, for which the city as now incorporated is liable.

The amount of the general city tax levied in 1854 was $342,000. Of this there was received into the Treasury, on the first Monday of January 1856, $292,195 67; leaving outstanding $49,804 33. The same tax for 1855 was $273,580; and on the same day there was collected $197,200, leaving outstanding $76.380.

On that day there was a cash balance in the Treasury of $68,362 07; of this sum $7,407 36, was credited to the general fund of 1853, and the balance to various local funds.

The assessments for local improvements during the year 1855 amount to $200,853. Of this sum $61,702 was for market grounds, and $62,000 for the opening of new streets.

A large amount of permanent improvements in the shape of paving, laying down sewers, extending gas and water pipes, and opening of new streets have been accomplished during the past year.

This work having been properly begun we are now enabled to carry out these and other works of public utility, co-temporaneously with the advance in our population, and the extension of our limits, thus avoiding future inconvenience and heavy expense in undoing the labor of previous time. The report of the City Surveyor for 1855 wi[ll] show that the number of miles of pave[d] streets in the City on the 1st day of January, 1856, was equal to 31¼. The number of miles of public sewerage was equal t[o] 34½. The number of miles of levels ru[n] recorded and entered in profile book durin[g] the two past years was 141⅓. This boo[k] shows the elevation of each street and sew er above ordinary water in Lake at inter vals of 100 feet. The number of linea[r] feet of sewer constructed during the pa[st] two years, was 21,276, or about four mile and cost $30,000. The whole number o[f] square feet of paving done during the pa[st] two years, equals 626,257 feet, at an ex pense including curbing and all other ston used of $132,620. The whole amount o[f] work staked out, calculated and reported b[y] that Department during the past two year was upwards of $130,000. Wherever thes improvements have been made, they hav enhanced the value of the lands for dwel[l] ings and business purposes far beyond th expense of their construction.

Real Estate.

Dealers in Real Estate inform us tha[t] the demand for lots, both improved an[d] unimproved, has been very active durin[g] the year, and this demand has been princi pally for a good class of dwellings, or desir able building lots; that sales of low price property, say under $200, have been belo[w] the average of the two years preceeding.

It would be impossible almost to give [a] complete list of the lots that have change[d] hands during the year, and even were i[t] possible to obtain them, want of space would preclude their insertion in this state ment. To give some idea, however, o[f] the class of buildings and lots that hav changed hands as well as to put on recor[d] where it may be afterwards referred to, th value of Real Estate in different parts o the city, we give the following list of som of the sales at auction made during th several months from March to December:

Brick house, lot 54 by 115, South Divis ion street near Cedar, 2,300.

3 wooden houses, lot 30 by 115, Swa[n] street near Cedar, 2,800.

1 brick house, lot 37 by 127, Eagle st near Michigan, 5,000.

1 brick house, lot 55 by 231, Main st. near Chippewa, 14,000.

1 wood house, lot 25 by 90, Ninth street near Carolina, 1,415.

1 brick house, lot 25 by 115, Swan st. near Pine, 2,124.

1 wood house, lot 25 by 179, Ellicott st. near Burton alley, 800.

1 wood house, lot 40 by 100, Eagle st. near Oak, 2,625.

2 wood houses, lot 50 by 60, Exchange street near Griffin, 1,273.

1 wood house, lot 50 by 200, Swan st. near Michigan, 6,000.

2 wood houses, lot 28 by 178, Swan st. near Chicago, 2,600.

1 brick house, lot 25 by 115, South Division st. near Oak, 3,000.

1 brick house, lot 25 by 115, South Division st. near Michigan, 2,450.

1 wood house, lot 25 by 70, Folsom st. near Chicago, 837.

1 brick house, lot 25 by 108, Swan st. near Pine, 2,700.

1 wood house, lot 31 by 132, Washington st. near Tupper, 1,450.

1 wood house, lot 18 by 100, Ninth st. near Maryland, 700.

1 brick house, lot 27 by 132, Franklin st. near Walden, 4,500.

1 brick house, lot 25 by 85, Virginia st. near Ninth, 2,050.

1 wood house, lot 29 by 115, Swan st. near Chestnut, 2,500.

1 wood house, lot 30 by 110, Pearl st. near Huron, 3,000.

On North street, corner of Franklin, 50 feet, to J. G. Deshler, at $30 per foot.

On North street, adjoining the above, 105½ feet to G. S. Hazard at the same price, and 100 feet to V. Tiphaine at $27 per foot.

On Delaware street, corner of Ferry, 153 by 200 feet, to Cyrus Clarke, at $35 per foot.

On Morgan street, corner of Huron, 43 feet, to S. M. Welch, for $47 per foot.

On Rock street, 175, feet from Genesee, to James T. Vandeventer, at $28 per foot.

On Sixth street, corner of Pennsylvania, 115 feet, to Philo Allen, at $15 per foot.

Eight lots adjoining on Sixth street. to Wm. Gray, Henry Smith, and Philo Allen. at $16 per foot.

On Pennsylvania street, adjoining the above, 50 feet, to Philo Allen, at $10 50 per foot.

On Twelfth street, corner of Pennsylvania, four lots sold to Henry Roop, at $10,25 per foot.

Eight lots adjoining, on Fifth street, to Henry Roop, at $9 75 per foot.

Lot on Swan st. 100 feet from Ellicott, 35 feet front, 115½ feet deep to the alley, at $85 per foot.

Lot on Swan st. 100 feet west of Spring st., 27 feet front, 120 feet deep, at $22 per foot, to A. A. Howard.

Three lots on Rose st. 112 feet south of North st. 25 feet front by 85 feet deep each $4 per foot, to G. B. Rich.

Two lots on North Jefferson st., Black Rock, 172½ feet north of Albany st., 25 feet front by 121 feet deep, each at $2 50 per foot, to O. F. Presbrey.

Two lots on Sherwood st. 105 feet north Hampshire st., 25 feet front by 121 feet deep, each at $2,25, to O. F. Presbrey.

Lot on west side of Rose st., 237 feet south of North st, 75 feet front by 100 feet deep, at $2,50 per foot, to James M. Baker.

Lot on east side of Seventh st., 50 feet south from Pennsylvania st, 27 feet front by 132 feet deep, at $14, per foot to A. A. Howard.

A block on north st. between Park st. and North William street, 268 feet front by 646 feet deep, sold by James Wadsworth to Dr. Walter Cary, for $20,000.—

A lot and dwelling on the corner of Delaware and Cary streets, sold for the benefit of the heirs of the late Eli Wilkeson, for $12,000 cash, to James M. Ganson, Esq.

A lot and dwelling on Delaware st. adjoining the residence of H. L. Lansing, Esq., sold by H. A. Gibson, to John Ganson, Esq., for $15,000.

A lot containing 16 acres on Elk st., about 3 miles from Main street, at $19,000 to Jesse Ketchum.

Two three story brick stores on Lloyd st. lot 40 by 60, at $12,000.

A two story brick dwelling on Virginia st. near Niagara, lot 25 by 86½, $2,665.— And small building lots and dwellings, ranging from $300 to $1000 each, parcel about $600.

6¼ acres of a lot containing 51 acres on Batavia street, a short distance east of the Williamsville road, at $225 per acre, and 6¼ acres at $250 per acre.

A lot 20 by 100 feet on Michigan, west side, 365 60-100 feet south of High st. with a one story frame house, for $29,50 per foot.

A lot 25 by 100 on Michigan st, west side, 415 50-100 feet south of High street with one story frame house at $29 per foot.

A lot 77 40-100 feet front, 33 feet rear, west line 68 feet, east line 98 feet on Batavia street, south side, 59 feet west of Oak street, at $21,50 per foot.

The houses and lots Nos. 1 and 2, in the southern end of the block on Washington st., were sold to Mr. W. H. Smith for $6,650, and $5,850 respectively.

No. 3 on Washington st. was bid in by W. C. Young, for the sum of $5,900.

No. 4 on the same street, was sold to W. O. Brown, for $6,400.

No. 5 on Ellicott st. was struck off to John R. Evans, for $2,600.

No. 6 on the same street, was bought by S. V. R. Watson for $2,400.

No. 7 on same street, was bid off by Joseph Stringham for $2,350.

Health of the City.

Buffalo in point of health will compare favorably with any other town in the country. The summer of 1854 was as notable for its dryness as that of '55 was for its wetness, and while the former was healthy the latter was even more so. When we consider the variableness of the weather during the past summer months, it is somewhat remarkable there was no prevailing sickness, and but little of the usual summer complaints.

By far the greater part of the streets are covered with excellent pavements which admit of their being kept perfectly clean; our location on a rising ground which enables us to obtain the most thorough sewerage, and which is carried out to the fullest extent, added to our superior position at the foot of Lake Erie where we enjoy the fresh breezes from the Lake, which serve to dispel all obnoxious vapors, are the causes, of our usual healthiness. We learn from the report of the health physician, that the number of deaths in 1855 was 1856. In 1854 there were 2,935, showing a decrease in 1855 of 1080 as compared with the previous year. The population of Buffalo at the close of 1855 as we have already stated, was probably not less than 80,000 The population of St. Louis at the close of the year was estimated at 130,000 and the number of deaths reported at 5,003.— Taking these two cities for the year 1855 and Baltimore, Philadelphia and New York for the year 1850 as returned in the U. S. Census, and Boston for a series of years we have the following result:

	Population.	No. Deaths.	Per Cent
Philadelphia	340,045	8,509	2,56
Baltimore	169,054	4,576	2,70
New York	515,547	22,702	4,43
Boston average per cent. of deaths for nine years			2,53
St. Louis, 1855	130,000	5,003	4,12
Buffalo	80,000	1,856	2,03

Common Schools.

The Common Schools of Buffalo are the best in the Union, and are the pride of our citizens. They are established upon that beneficient principle which entitles the child of the humblest citizen to educational facilities equal to that of the son of the millionaire. An excellent system of free education in a city like Buffalo, cannot fail to entail blessings on the rising generation which can only be estimated on the broadest principles of political economy, Strangers visiting our city are forcibly struck with the stately edifices that are used for Common School purposes, and which rear their walls in every quarter of the city. Within these buildings an army of over 20,000 children selected from all classes of society, have been taught during the past year those salutary lessons of instruction which shall determine their future characters, and which are to make them good citizens and useful members of society.

The State tax for the Public School Fund amounts to $800,000. The amount apportioned to this county was $23,813 55. Buffalo paid of the school tax $16,797 32 while the twenty four towns paid out $7,016 23.

The Superintendent of schools in his annual report says:

"One third of the $23,813 55 raised, or $7,937 85, we will consider is distributed in is county, according to law, by districts the three hundred and twenty districts Erie county, each will receive of the ,937 85, the sum of $24 80, and the enty-nine districts of the city receive only 19 20, while the two hundred and ninety e districts in the towns receive more than ı times as much, or $7,218 65. One ird of what Buffalo pays, is $5,599 10; nsequently she looses on this amount by is mode of distribution, $4,879,90. Of e remaining two-thirds Buffalo pays $11,- '8 21; but as this is distributed according population, she receives only $7,823 48,)sing thereby $3,376 18; thus making an gregate loss to the city, or a tax for the nefit of the country towns of $8,256 08. s an offset to this loss, we receive a pro- ertion of about $300,000, annual income ɔm the common school fund; but the ıole amount from this source and from e $800,000 State tax, was but $12,988,-). Our proportion paid of the $800,000 ene, being $16,797 32, we pay $3,808 52 ore than we receive from both these urces. In short, the city supports its hools by direct taxation, looses its entire oportion of the income of the common hool fund, and, besides contributes $3,-)8 52 towards the support of the county hools."

This furnishes a very strong argument · the formation of a new county including ly the present city limits, and we sincere- trust that this project which is now before e Common Council, will be carried out. 'om the Mayor's Message we learn that e number of teachers of all grades in the blic schools of the city during the past ar was 180, and the number of children attendance is over 20,000. The common ools cost the city last year apart from the pense of new buildings, repairs, &c., the m of $80,000.

Harbor Facilities.

The harbor of Buffalo is constituted by e mouth of Buffalo Creek, which has elve to fourteen feet of water for the dis- ice of a mile from its mouth, with an erage width of two hundred feet and is otected by a substantial stone pier and ı wall jutting out into the Lake, at the d of which there is a lighthouse twenty feet in diameter by forty-six feet in height. A ship canal seven hundred yards long, eighty feet wide and thirteen deep has been constructed, running nearly parallel with the creek, and about midway between the creek and the Lake, as a further accommodation for vessels. The extension of the Erie Canal a mile to the eastward of its original terminus, and the construction of side cuts and slips for the accommodation of canal boats has considerably increased the harbor room. The city authorities have also ex- pended large sums in the excavation of ship canals and slips, connecting the creek with the main ship canal, and with the Erie canal. Two large canal basins, the Ohio and Erie as they have been named, have been constructed under the auspices of the State. These basins have been used by canal boats and lumber vessels principally, thereby increasing the capacity of the main harbor for the larger class of Lake ship- ping.

The works erected by the United States for the improvement of the harbor consists of a sea wall along the Lake shore for near- ly a mile in length, a channel pier of about six hundred and fifty feet and a mole of about sixteen hundred feet long, The south pier or mole was so much injured during the great gale of October, 1844, as to make it necessary to rebuild the parapet wall. The old wall was constructed of small materials and was but two feet thick. In 1845 it was decided to rebuild it in a more sub- stantial manner. The new wall is built of heavy stone, averaging four feet in length and weighing from one to three tons, dress- ed on the beds and joints, leaving a rough or rock face, and well laid in hydraulic ce- ment; it is eight feet wide at the bottom and is gradually reduced to four feet at the top and crowned by a heavy coping one foot thick. The foundation extends below the low water line and is ten feet wide, formed of large masses of stone laid in cement. The top of the wall is level, about 16 feet above the lake, of 11 feet width and about 1,500 feet in length. In 1845 the new work was commenced, but was suspended in 1846 from want of funds. In 1852 an appropria- tion of $14,000 was made and the work was resumed in 1853. During 1853 and 1854 there were reconstructed about one thousand feet of the exterior slope of an average width of about twelve feet, 1000 feet of the top covered with a broad flagging; over four hundred feet of the parapet wall raised 5½ feet and completed; some three hundred feet of the old wall removed, excavations made, and a new wall built completing the parapet wall within the amount appropriated for that purpose. The excavations and removal of the old stone wall in 1853-4, for the foundation of the new amounted to over 3,000 cubic yards, and the mass of stone used in the work done to over 5,000 cubic yards. An appropriation of $35,000 or $40,000 will be required to take up the Quay wall which is now in a dilapidated state and rebuild it of heavy materials, in the same style as the parapet wall, and also to dredge the channel between the piers. This sum would complete the present harbor in a permanent and thorough manner. The south pier should be at once extended into deeper water, to obviate in some degree the difficulty of entrance now experienced in consequence of the injudicious location of the Erie Basin breakwater. For some years past a bar has been forming at the entrance to the creek, which has prevented vessels entering the harbor, drawing over ten feet water. The extension of the south pier, it is thought, would keep this channel free.— During the past season the city appropriated $2,000, and our business men contributed $5,000 more which was expended in removing this bar, and we have now a channel of sufficient depth of water to admit of the heaviest draft vessels on the Lakes with a full cargo, entering the harbor in the severest gales with perfect safety.

During the past year private enterprize has done a great deal towards increasing the facilities of our harbor. New slips and a very large amount of docking have been constructed. Although we have a continuous dock of over a mile in length on the north side of the creek, and a large number of docks on the ship canal, canal slips, side cuts and basins, they are still inadequate to the wants of a growing commerce like that of Buffalo. On the Erie Basin during the past year two slips capable of accommodating a large number of the largest class of steamers, or propellers, have been constructed besides several side c Some five or six steam dredges were k constantly at work excavating, and at eighteen hundred feet of new docking been built on the Coit slip. When c pleted it will be a work of magnificent portions creditable to the commercial cl acter and position of Buffalo, and materially enhance not only the value, the general appearance of property in t portion of the city. On the Pratt & W ham's slip, and on the creek and ship ca about 700 feet of new docking were b last summer, and the proprietors into building some two thousand feet more They will also erect during the com season a large warehouse on these premi Another slip is also in contemplation c ting through from the creek to the s canal in the rear of the premises on wh these docks have been constructed. Th are only some of the most important vate enterprises prosecuted during the p year demanded by our augmented tra As our business increases, our facilities its greater dispatch increase in like prop tion.

More than this, however, is required meet the demands of the large and gro ing commerce of our port, and it is conte plated to open a new channel from t Lake to the creek at above a miles dista from its mouth, across the isthmus, wh is not above two hundred and fifty ya in width, and this improvement with erection of a new break water, and facilities there are for building docks on slips and ship canals would render the h bor sufficiently capacious to accommod the increase in the shipping of the port some years to come.

With the growth of Buffalo as a gr market—until she has gained the repu tion of being the "Greatest grain market this continent," facilities for handling t the great number of cargoes that are da arriving during the season of navigation h kept pace with the commerce. In 1825 a for many subsequent years, all the grain c goes were handled in buckets, and from th days to a week were consumed in dischar ing a single cargo, during which the ves would on an average lose one or two f winds. Now the largest cargoes are rea discharged by steam in fewer hours than days at that time. During one evening .st summer, a fair wind brought a large :et into port, and about dusk nearly 600,- 00 bushels of grain were afloat in our harbor, and in less than 36 hours thereafter very bushel had been put in store, and a .rge portion of the vessels reloaded and .eared for the Upper Lake. There is no ort in the world where like facilities are fforded for storing an equal amount in he same time. And yet no one at he time supposed from appearances that nything unusual was going on. This ex-edition is owing to the large number of Elevators that have been erected in our arbor from time to time by our enterprizing citizens. There are at present in good working order on the creek ten Elevators capable of elevating and storing without iny crowding, the following quantities of rain:

	Capacity.	Per hour.
'ity Elevator	350,000 bush.	2,500 bush.
Iatch's	200,000 "	2,500 "
Evans's	200,000 "	2,500 "
Fish's	150,000 "	2,500 "
Seymour & Wells'	150,000 "	2,500 "
Dart's	150,000 "	2,000 "
Sterling's	140,000 "	2,000 "
Buffalo	80,000 "	2,500 "
Johnson's	80,000 "	2,500 "
Hollister's	50,000 "	1,400 "
	1,550,000 "	22,400 "

Several of these elevators possess facilities for loading canal boats twice as fast as they can elevate from a vessel's hold, and two of them, the City and Fish's are so connected with the freight depot of the New York Central Railroad, that cars are run to either of them, and are as easily loaded as canal boats in the slips would be.

A new Elevator is just now being built by J. G. Deshler and Capt. M. Hazard, on the corner of the Peck slip and the creek, and almost immediately opposite the foot of Main Street, which it is contemplated will be ready for the fall business. This building will cost about $70,000. Is to be furnished with two Elevators, and is estimated to hold about 400,000 bushels.— Excavations for another Elevator on the west side of the creek nearly opposite the foot of Lloyd street, have been commenced. It is designed to be of the capacity of about 500,000 bushels, and to have two elevators, one on the creek and one on the cut, each capable of raising 4,000 bushels per hour. These two elevators will add 900,000 bu. to the capacity of the elevators in the harbor, making an aggregate of 2,450,000 bushels. Since the two large transportation companies have decided to move their offices, and use the docks in the Erie Basin, a proposition has been made to build still another Elevator on the north side of Peacock slip Erie Basin. This, however, has not been definitely settled upon. Several additions and improvements have been made to the elevators already built during the past year, the most important of which is the addition to the Evans elevator of a brick building 75 feet front by 80 feet deep on the Evans slip, and four stories high, and the building of a second elevating apparatus to the Hatch elevator.

There are also to be found in our harbor some seven or eight tugs which render important service in hauling vessels up and down the creek, bringing them in when they are becalmed in the bay, or when in distress out side. They are a very valuable addition to our harbor facilities, and could not well be dispensed with.

Banks and Banking.

Below we present a statement of the condition of the several City Banks on the 31st December, 1855, as appears by their quarterly reports, published in accordance to law. From this table it will be seen that the aggregate Capital, which was, in 1854, $2,191,800, has decreased $17,000, and was, at the close of the past year, $2,174,800—the Pratt Bank, an individual concern, having reduced its capital $20,000, while Whites' have increased theirs $3,000. An effort was made last Fall to start another Bank, but the attempt was unsuccessful. Several of our Banks, among whom we have heard mentioned the Marine, O. Lee & Co.'s, Buffalo City, and others, contemplate increasing their capital this winter by several hundred thousand dollars. The capital of the former, we are told, will be increased from $300,000 to $500,000.

More than this, however, is required to meet the wants of our large and growing trade and commerce. The banking facilities of our city, as we have before remarked, are wholly disproportioned to the amount of business here annually transacted. The entire resources of all the Banks now located here, to say nothing of the resources of a large number of other Banks scattered throughout the interior of the State, are inadequate to the wants of the produce and forwarding business alone. The discounts to produce and forwarding houses are made on ten and fifteen day paper, payable in New York, and the Banks, as a natural consequence, having as much of this class of paper as they wish, prefer this business to that of manufacturers and those in other branches of trade, who make their paper on longer time and payable at home. By thus renewing their discounts at so short intervals, and each time receiving the benefit of exchange between this city and New York, the Banks are enabled to make large profits. We know of no city where a Bank of large capital could more profitably be located than in Buffalo. Such an institution, with a capital of not less than one million of dollars, which would confine its operations to discounting paper, payable at home or in Western cities, charging seven per cent interest and a quarter or half per cent for collecting Western paper, taking Western money at par and paying out the same to its manufacturing customers, would confer more real benefits on our city than are gained by the present practice. Such an institution will never be found in our city until our manufacturers and tradesmen take hold and start it, and then control it. They must be content to take small profits, and must not seek to swell them by shifts and evasions of the statutes against usury.

From the table which follows it will be seen that the "loans and discounts" of all the Banks on the 31st December last for the quarter was $5,243,440, or an increase over the same period in 1854 of $1,277,553 99, and the profits on the 31st December, 1855, were $271,597 04, or an increase over the same period in 1854 of $55,466 63. The amount of specie at the close of the year was only $49,349 77, showing a decrease, as compared with the year previous, of $29,164 66, and in the amount of notes in circulation the table below shows it to be for December last $1,175,087, an increase ov 1854 of $330,102. The amount on depo was $1,779,161 38, or an increase over t year previous of $443,476 18.

We also learn that the amount of sight e change sold in our city during the year e ceeded $25,000,000.

Exchange on New York in this city h ruled throughout the year at from ¼ to ½ p cent.

There are some thirty-two or thirty-thr Broker or exchange offices located in o city which do not carry on a legitimate ban ing, but who, nevertheless, receive on depos from our merchants, and who do annually a enormous amount of business. Amon these we might notice, as the most prom nent, John R. Lee & Co., Brown & Co., Rol inson & Co., H. Johnson, S. P. Stokes & Co Budd & Thayer, E. S. Dann & Co., Honli tein & Montgomery, &c. The amount o business annually transacted by this class o banking institutions, could it be ascertaine would compare favorably in profits, as well a extent, with that done by our regular Bank

There are also located in our city fou Savings' Banks, viz: the Buffalo Saving Bank, Erie County Savings Bank, Wester Savings Bank, and the Buffalo Trust Com pany. These institutions are all in a ver flourishing condition, and have conferred in calculable benefits on a large class of our citi zens.

The following table will show the condi tion of the several Banks of Buffalo, on th the 31st day of December, 1855, as appear by their quarterly statements, which are re quired to be made and published by the law of our State:

	RESOURCES.	
Bank of Attica. Buffalo City Bank. Fa's and Mec's Bank. Hollister Bank. International Bank. Marine Bank. New York and Erie Bank. O. Lee & Co's Bank. Pratt Bank. Sackett's Harbor Bank. White's Bank.		NAME OF BANK.
Total.		
576,034 86 401,746 17 327,471 55 549,271 84 674,867 63 690,356 69 376,400 24 644,327 25 68,988 79 390,085 57 543,890 24		Loans and Discounts.
$5,243,440 74		

THE CITY OF BUFFAO.

These sums are included in "Loans and Discounts."

LIABILITIES.

NAME OF BANK.	Capital.	Profits.	Bank Note Circulation.	Due Treasurer State of N. Y.	Due Depositors.	Due Banks on Demand.	Due Individuals and Corporations.	Due to all Others.	Total.
Bank of Attica	160,000 00	20,651 37	101,619 00	45,074 83	206,666 12	72,611 91	---	44,074 64	711,757 87
Buffalo City Bank	204,900 00	38,317 42	103,157 00	40,450 95	95,142 81	---	31,648 59	62,503 19	579,654 45
Far's and Mec's Bank	100,000 00	4,354 79	80,028 00	60,920 19	166,674 02	1,633 68	41,469 74	41,684 94	462,787 87
Hollister Bank	200,000 00	41,531 57	91,594 00	60,926 27	217,290 68	54,744 26	---	---	707,510 07
International Bank	400,000 00	46,193 81	138,000 00	73,185 54	169,139 00	69,460 36	---	---	896,787 91
Marine Bank	300,000 00	26,397 00	127,066 00	73,935 91	266,369 42	102,441 85	3,511 30	984 22	891,407 14
New York & Erie Bank	200,000 00	17,679 65	99,399 00	60,295 75	95,249 21	44,061 66	---	---	524,357 09
O. Lee & Co.'s Bank	170,000 00	24,065 40	80,900 00	248,705 03	195,226 01	44,186 42	---	25,146 82	835,709 65
Pratt Bank	40,000 00	8,347 14	53,791 00	85,254 82	10,036 49	---	---	---	177,382 77
Sackett's Harbor Bank	200,000 00	16,204 97	190,308 00	42,464 72	108,257 85	15,461 50	41,469 74	---	562,088 04
White's Bank	200,000 00	27,640 46	109,385 00	87,298 63	212,792 97	70,491 02	71,241 24	---	773,207 31
Total	$2,174,900 00	$271,397 04	$1,175,087 00	$863,881 60	$1,779,161 38	$730,971 00	$147,700 67	$285,739 08	$7,122,650 77

Bonds and Mortgages.	50,317 00 / 50,124 00 / 54,917 83 / 47,431 00 / 50,254 18 / 73,081 00 / 68,440 84 / 524,357 09 / 50,468 00 / 27,700 47 / 27,652 75 / 14,790 58 / 63,800 00	
Stocks.	65,624 10 / 85,201 55 / 69,000 00 / 61,900 00 / 80,000 00 / 57,761 70 / 93,000 00 / 29,000 00 / 53,334 25 / 94,575 00	
Loss and Expense Account.	864 97 / 6,81 68 / 546 60 / 7,939 29 / 1,182 84 / 1,108 25 / 2,593 08	
Over Drafts.	1,784 92 / 3,274 13 / 4,322 73 / 1,471 42 / 1,939 98 / 2,622 87 / 5,944 12 / 21,861 82 / 6,038 00 / 13,172 69 / 3,150 21 / 5,881 21 / 8,793 37	
Specie.	4,452 70 / 5,009 55 / 2,921 61 / 4,934 94 / 4,042 61 / 8,294 23 / 3,045 38 / 6,038 00 / 1,151 85 / 5,881 21 / 3,577 66	
Cash Items.	4,414 40 / 1,938 73 / 70 20 / 1,471 60 / 7,232 25 / 5,730 14 / 13,172 69 / 3,672 50 / 4,217 02 / 30,117 21	
Bills of Solvent Banks on hand.	2,799 63 / 7,063 00 / 6,593 00 / 20,354 00 / 6,187 00 / 4,200 00 / 11,606 73 / 6,085 00 / 2,987 00 / 2,350 00 / 11,283 00 / 10,190 00	
Due from Banks.	2,461 39 / 5,715 64 / 14,398 85 / 19,324 95 / 50,187 25 / 11,606 73 / 6,085 00 / 12,000 00 / 1,915 33 / 50,265 81 / 18,203 63	
Real and Personal Estate.	10,664 37 / 7,500 00 / 32,852 27 / 26,340 25	
Due from Directors.	12,500 00 / 2,024 50 / *64,786 19 / 13,300 00 / *24,511 84 / *3,000 00	
Due from Brokers.	171 65	
Bills of Suspended Banks on hand.	74 00	
Office Furniture, Plate, &c.	3,675 19 / 1,362 09	
Due from Railroad Corporations.	4,366 62	

State of Trade.

The year through which we have just passed has been an unusually prosperous one throughout the whole country, and especially so in our own city. Other cities, it is true, have, to a certain extent, been affected by disturbances in the monetary world, but these have been few, and as a general thing have acted as healthful checks upon speculation, inducing caution and prudence, where the absence of these qualities might have resulted otherwise. In our city, during the year, nothing happened to impair the confidence in our business men—all their engagements have been promptly met, and the operations of the year have been more than usually successful.

For the first time in many years the balance of trade between this country and Europe was in our favor, by several millions of dollars. The occasional panics which occurred during the year, in addition to operating as a check upon importations, were valuable also in bringing out unmistakably the strong and healthful basis on which the general prosperity of the country rests. The present prosperous condition of our country may undoubtedly be traced to the productive resources of the West, to the large surplus of the necessaries of life which the year produced, and which remain over from previous years, and to the demand which existed for these articles, both at home and abroad. The Western States have sent forward, during the past year, a very large surplus of their products, and, in return, the farmers have obtained an equivalent, mostly in cash; in fact we doubt whether they have ever received higher prices for their grain and provisions, and have therefore been enabled to enlarge their farms and increase their facilities for greater productions the coming season.

As a general thing our people are out of debt, and have an abundance of means besides to carry forward their operations for the year. Our merchants find but little difficulty in making their collections, and are, consequently, enabled to meet their own paper at maturity. With an abundance of money in the hands of the producing classes; with but a moderate amount of indebtedness on the part of our merchants; with an immense surplus of breadstuffs in the country, and provisions more than can be needed to supply the wants of our own people, with abundant facilities for transporting these surplus products to market and with an entire certainty that they will be wanted, we are constrained to congratulate our citizens upon the present prosperous condition of our country, as well as upon what there is every reason for believing the future has in store for us.

Our Railroads, shipping and the canals will have all that they can do to move the surplus productions of the West to market during the coming year. Labor will be in demand and money abundant. Should occasional disturbances come, either through monetary revulsions in Europe or at commercial centres here, the country is in too sound a condition to admit of more than a brief duration. We therefore feel that the year upon which we have just entered—at least the indications are such—will be even more prosperous than the one we have just passed through.

Flour.

The receipts of flour during the past year show a very large increase over 1854. For several years past our imports of flour by Lake have shown a gradual but steady decrease until 1855, when it will be seen that the increase was 197,412 bbls. This decrease is to be accounted for in that there was a short crop in 1854, and from the fact that new routes have put forth every exertion by reducing the rates of transportation and sending agents into the western country to contract for forwarding by these routes to secure a portion of this trade, believing that when once their line was known and established, it would draw trade of itself, and they would then be enabled to raise their tariff of prices. That they have in a measure succeeded is beyond a doubt. Our market has now become so well established, and from the fact that prices as a general thing, rule higher here than in New York, less the cost of transportation, our receipts must continue to increase with each year unless there should be a large falling off in the crop which would in that event affect the receipts at all the other Lake ports.

The receipts during the past four years compare as follows:

1852..........bbls. 1,299,513, 1854..............739,811
1853..................983,837, 1855..............937,223

Included in the above receipts are 67,000 bbls. which have been received from Canada

...ortion of it by Lake, and the remainder ne over the Buffalo and Brantford Rail-.d, and was brought to this city by the ry boat belonging to that road.

Our receipts, therefore, for the past year uld foot up as follows:

Lake from Western States,	870,223 bbls	
" Canada	40,000	
Buffalo & Brantford Railroad	27,000	937,223
State Line Railroad		66,683
ufactured at Black Rock		175,000
Mills in the City and Vicinity		5,000
Total		1,183,906

his amount has been disposed of as follows:

ped by Canal from Buffalo	235,578 bbls
" " " " Black Rock	99,017 "
v York Central Railroad	475,000 "
Falo & New York City Railroad	185,628 "
pped to Canada and Tonawanda by river	25,000 "
sumed in City	88,683 "
ount in store at close of navigation	75,000 "
Total	1,183,906

These figures are in part estimated, but believe they would vary but little from e actual result could it be arrived at.

Notwithstanding the large increase in r receipts this year, the shipments by nal show a considerable falling off as compared with the year previous.

al shipments in 1854 were	288,124	bbls.
" " 1855 were	235,578	"
Decrease in 1855	52,546	"

The following will show the quantity of ur manufactured by the several mills now operation at Black Rock, during the past ee years:

	1853.	1854.	1855.
e Mills	70,000 bbls.	68,705	52,000
gara Mills	65,000 "	60,000	58,000
ntier Mills	34,429 "	22,511	2,000
en City Mills	33,867 "	35,992	32,000
ton Mills	20,000 "	15,000	21,000
be Mills	12,000 "	11,000	10,000
	235,296 "	213,208	175,000

The Frontier Mills which were destroyed fire in December, 1853, have been re-ilt, but have not as yet ground any large ount of wheat. This fact, together with e high price of wheat last season, has occasioned the decrease in the amount of flour unfactured during the year.

There has been an active demand for ur during the past year, and the market ened in the spring at a considerable advance over the current rates of the spring 1854, and maintained the advance during the earlier part of the season. The ck of old wheat was very nearly exhausted at the close of 1854, so that on the opening of navigation in 1855 there was very little remaining in first hands, or in store to come forward and what there was, was as a general thing of a very inferior quality. The uncertainty attending the success of the coming crop, which was feared might prove a failure, added to the belief that there would be a large foreign demand, contributed to enhance the value of both wheat and flour, and kept back much that would otherwise have come into market. Later in the season, when it became evident that there was to be a large crop, and before it had been damaged by the continued rains during harvest, prices began to decline. By the table which we give below it will be seen that the highest prices prevailed during the months of May, June and July, while the closing prices of the year show no material variation from those of 1854.

A very marked improvement was apparent in the various brands of flour received last year from the upper lakes. The flour from Michigan, and which has always hitherto stood high in this market, was nearly all made from grown wheat last season, and was, comparatively speaking, but little sought after.

Nearly all the flour which was received at this port last year, prior to the new crop, came from Lake Michigan, and was controlled by one or two parties who had gone into the market and purchased a large proportion of the wheat and flour that came to Wisconsin ports on that Lake during the fall and winter—this to a certain extent served to keep up the high prices which ruled in the early part of the summer. The demand for flour about the close of canal navigation to supply the interior of our State was unusually brisk, but was suddenly checked by the announcement that the New York Central Railroad would not transport flour or produce of any description to any way station on their line, until all the through freight in their depots, and that sent them from day to day to be shipped to New York was all forwarded. This decision on the part of the managers of that road, resulted injuriously to the interests of many of our produce merchants, and compelled buyers who were in this market from interior towns, to procure their supplies in other quarters. Again at the close of canal navigation the roads put up their tariff so high that it almost amounted to a prohibition in sending forward by these channels, and not content with this, they have made their contracts with parties in Ohio and other Western States, to transport every description of produce to New York and deliver it at considerably below the rates which the same property would pay were it shipped to Buffalo and thence re-shipped to New York, thereby descriminately in favor of New York and western merchants to the injury of our own city.

Buffalo, as a Flour market, is becoming more and more important, each year.— Within a few years a trade has sprung up with the interior towns of our own State, as well as with the adjoining counties in Pennsylvania, and with several of the New England States, which carries off a large amount of flour annually, and which demand is increasing every year, as these districts which look to us for their supplies become more populated, and as they find it to their interests to purchase here.

Of the amount of flour received at this port during the year, between 6 and 700,000 bbls. changed hands in our market. Scarcely a month passes, but some new line of Rail Road extending through rich and flourishing portions of the Western States is opened, which brings their surplus products to a market at upper Lake ports, and which finally reach this point to be sold or forwarded to New York or other seaboard markets.

The table which we give below shows the quotations for good to choice brands of flour during the season. The large number of brands and grades of flour received in this market renders it a difficult matter to give a complete and accurate table of prices; but we believe the following may be relied on as the average of prices obtained for the several descriptions noted:

Months.	Days	1855.		1854.	
May	11	$9,50	to 9,75	$8 50	to 8,62½
May	18	9,75	to 10,00	8 37½	to 8,62½
May	25	9,87½	to 10,00	8 37½	to 8,56½
June	1	9,50	to 9,87½	8 50	to 8,75
June	8	9,75	to 10,00	8 75	to 9,00
June	15	9,75	to 10,00	8 56¼	to 9,00
June	22	9,62½	to 9,75	8 00	to 8,50
June	29	9,50	to 9,75	7 25	to 7,50
July	6	9,25	to 9,50	7 50	to 7,75
July	13	9,25	to 9,50	7 25	to 7,75
July	20	8,87	to 9,25	7 50	to 7,75
July	27	8,75	to 9,25	7 62½	to 7,75
August	3	8,50	to 9,00	8 00	to 8,50
August	10	8,50	to 8,75	8 00	to 8,25
August	17	8,50	to 8,75	8 25	to 8,50
August	24	7,75	to 8,00	9 00	to 9,37½
August	31	7,50	to 7,75	9,00	to 9,37½
September	7	6,50	to 6,75	8,75	to 9,00
September	14	7,00	to 7,50	8,50	to 8,75
September	21	7,37½	to 7,50	8 00	to 8,25
September	28	7,25	to 7,37	7 00	to 7,25
October	5	7,12	to 7,37	6 50	to 6,87½
October	12	7,75	to 8,00	7 62½	to 7,87½
October	19	7,56	to 8,00	7 75	to 8,00
October	26	7,75	to 8,75	8 00	to 8,50
November	2	8,75	to 9,00	8 25	to 8,50
November	9	8,50	to 8,75	8 50	to 8,62½
November	16	7,87	to 8,00	8 50	to 8,75
November	23	8,50	to 9,00	8 62½	to 8,75
November	30	9,00	to 9,12	8 75	to 8,82½

Wheat.

The receipts of wheat during the past year show an enormous increase over 1854. The quantity received by Lake during the past four years was as follows:

```
1852..........bu 5,549,778   1854..........bu 3,510,79?
1853..........bu 5,424,043   1855..........bu 8,016,82?
```

Here we have an increase last year of 4,566,029 bushels. In 1853 the high prices brought out all the surplus wheat in the country, leaving barely sufficient for seed. This, added to a short crop in 1854 made the receipts of that year fall below the average of a number of years. Of the receipts of 1855 over three fourths were of the crop of that year, and did not begin to come forward until September.

It will be seen, by reference to our tables in another part of the review, that the receipts from Canada last year, under the Reciprocity Treaty, were nearly 500,000 bushels, or an increase, as compared with 1854, of about 345,853 bushels.

The receipts last year, so far as we have been able to learn, were disposed of as follows:

```
Shipped by Canal.............................bu 6,455,641
Shipped to Canada, Oswego, Black Rock and
   Tonawanda..................................bu   700,000
Shipped by Railroad..........................bu   200,000
Consumed by City Mills.......................bu   121,180
In Store at close of Navigation..............bu   600,000
                                                ─────────
   Total....................................... 8,076,821
```

This estimate we believe to be correct, although by some it is contended that the amount we have put down as shipped by Railroad is too small.

Of the amount shipped by Canal, 478,589 bushels were left at Black Rock for milling.

As was the case with flour, the bulk of

the receipts of wheat prior to the new crop were consigned to one or two firms in our city, who controlled the market and kept prices up. Nearly the whole of this wheat was from Lake Michigan ports. The receipts of white wheat from Michigan and Ohio last year were rather light and the quality inferior, caused by the rains during harvest.

Shortly after the opening of navigation, several cargoes of upper Lake wheat, which were detained on the flats and frozen in above Detroit, were brought down before the Straits were open, and were readily taken up, at figures considerably above those of the fall before, when it was shipped.

The market for wheat has, during the last season, ruled very high. The average rates have been considerably above those in 1854, and the market has been fully sustained throughout the year. Millers from the interior of our State have been constantly in our market, and have purchased largely to supply their mills. The lowest limit touched during the season was towards the close of August and beginning of September, when it was anticipated that an abundant new crop might seriously depress prices, and buyers, therefore, were extremely cautious. The damage which resulted from wet harvest weather soon proving to be more disastrous than at first anticipated, the market immediately rallied, and from that forward continued firm and active, at good prices. The announcement of the short crop in Europe, and the large purchases in Western markets on foreign account, also served to keep prices up to the highest pitch.

Of the large amount received by Lake, nearly the whole of it was on Buffalo account, or sent here to be sold, and the proportion of that consigned through was very small. Of the eight million bushels received, from two-thirds to three-quarters changed hands in this market.

The following table will show the average prices of white Ohio and Michigan, red do. and Upper Lake Wheat, once a week during the season, in the Buffalo market, for the years 1854 and 1855:

Month	Day	1855. White	Red	Upper Lake	1854. White	Red	Upper Lake
May	11	$2 25	2 00	1 90	2 08	....	1 63
May	18	2 25	2 00	1 90	2 12	....	1 66
May	25	2 30	2 44	1 90	2 12½	....	1 67
June	1	2 40	2 10	1 95	2 13	....	1 67
June	8	2 40	2 20	1 85	2 19	....	....
June	15	2 37	....	1 85	2 08	....	....
June	22	2 30	....	1 80	2 00	....	....
June	29	2 35	....	1 70	1 90	....	1 25
July	6	2 30	....	1 78	1 80	....	1 10
July	13	2 30	....	1 75	1 78	....	1 10
July	20	2 30	1 80	1 75	1 85	1 65	....
July	27	2 25	1 80	1 60	1 87½	....	....
August	3	2 25	1 68	1 50	1 89	....	....
August	10	2 23	....	1 55	1 80	1 50	1 50
August	17	1 87	1 62	1 55	1 80	1 65	....
August	24	1 85	1 50	1 45	1 83	....	....
August	31	1 90	1 58	....	1 90	1 80	....
September	7	....	....	....	1 80	1 66	1 65
September	14	1 75	1 50	1 40	1 30	1 70	1 50
September	21	1 75	....	1 46	1 76	1 60	1 30
September	28	1 85	....	1 50	....	1 35	1 20
October	5	1 88	....	1 50	1 54	....	1 20
October	12	1 95	....	1 70	1 77	1 62	1 37
October	19	2 05	....	1 66	1 90	....	1 40
October	26	....	....	1 70	2 05	....	....
November	2	....	....	1 75	2 00	1 85	1 60
November	9	1 95	1 75	1 70	2 00	1 68	....
November	16	....	....	1 70	1 96	1 70	....
November	22	....	....	1 80	2 00	1 75	1 50
November	30	2 12½	....	1 80	2 00	....	1 50

Corn.

The receipts of Corn during the past season show a considerable falling off, as compared with the previous year. The corn crop of 1854, from which the supply of the past year has been received, was almost a failure, owing to excessive drought, and the surplus in the corn growing States was hardly worth speaking about. The crop of 1855 is said to be the largest ever raised in the West, and from this the supply of the coming season is to be derived. As none of last year's crop has come forward, we may confidently predict an enormous increase in our receipts during the coming season.

The receipts for the past four years foot up as follows:

1852.............bu 5,136,746   1854.............bu 10,109,973
1853.............bu 3,665,793   1855.............bu 8,722,516

Showing a decrease in 1855 of 1,387,457 bushels.

The receipts during the year have been disposed of as follows:

Bushels.
Amount Shipped by Canal..................7,713,451
    "   "   to Canada...................100,700
    "   "   by Railroad...................100,000
    "   in Store at close of Navigation.........200,000
    "   used by Distillers and for feed..........608,365

Total..................8,722,516

The market for corn during the past year was quite active, and the demand was at all times fully equal to the supply, though frequently checked by the high prices asked.

Prices of corn in this market ruled higher than was ever before known. The highest figure reached was about the close of the month of May, and from that time forward throughout the season, until the close of canal navigation, the most liberal prices continued to be paid, the market closing at about 15 cents advance on the quotations of 1854.

The corn received last year was unusually sound. For several years past the corn from Toledo has been heated, and that received in the early part of the season has been invariably unsound. Last year this was not the case, and the Toledo corn brought as high prices as the Chicago. Of the large amount received last year, nearly all was on Buffalo account, and changed hands in our market. Below, in connection with oats, we give a range of prices for the past three years.

Oats.

The receipts of Oats, as well as Corn, show a large falling off in 1855. The crop of 1854 was very much less than the average, and the receipts during the early part of the season were light from this cause;— Owing to the high prices of Wheat and Corn there is less disposition on the part of farmers to engage in the cultivation of Oats, and very many barely raise sufficient for their own use.

The receipts for the past four years foot up as follows:

	Bushels.		Bushels.
1852	2,596,231	1854	4,475,618
1853	1,480,655	1855	2,683,123

Or a decrease in 1855, as compared with 1854, of 1,792,495 bushels.

The receipts for the year were disposed of as follows:

	Bushels.
Shipped by Canal	2,287,950
" to Canada	50,000
In Store at close of Navigation	150,000
City Consumption	195,173
Total	2,683,123

Oats have been in active request during the whole season, and all that were offered found a ready market, and the supply at times was far from meeting the wants of the trade for local consumption. The market opened high at the commencement of the season, owing to light stock remaining from the crop of 1854, and continued very firm until September, when prices fell off, and closed quite dull at a decline of 20 cents from the opening prices in the Spring.

The following table will show the average prices of Corn and Oats, once a week during the business season, in the Buffalo market, for the years 1853, 1854 and 1855:

Month	Day	1853 Corn	1853 Oats	1854 Corn	1854 Oats	1855 Corn	1855 Oats
May	11	52c	40c	60c	44c	93c	60c
May	18	53c	41c	54c	45c	95½c	61c
May	25	55c	41c	59c	44c	95c	62c
June	1	54c	39c	62½c	45c	90c	65c
June	8	52c	38c	65c	44½c	88c	63c
June	15	52c	35c	65c	44½c	80c	53c
June	22	51c	35c	67c	43½c	85c	50c
June	29	50c	33c	60c	42½c	74c	56c
July	6	52c	32c	55c	42c	76c	55c
July	13	52½c	32c	53c	39c	80c	55c
July	20	57c	35c	54c	35c	79c	53c
July	27	61c	36c	58½c	35c	77c	50c
August	3	65c	40c	59c	36c	72c	48c
August	10	65c	38c	59c	34c	74c	48c
August	17	62c	38c	61½c	35c	75c	45c
August	24	62½c	36c	69c	43½c	78c	46c
August	31	62½c	36c	65½c	40c	76c	46c
September	7	65c	35c	65½c	42c	73½c	32c
September	14	66c	35c	67c	43½c	73c	32½c
September	21	65c	34c	67c	43½c	74c	34c
September	28	63c	34c	64½c	42c	74½c	35½c
October	5	68c	34c	61c	42c	73c	37c
October	12	66c	35c	67c	43c	83c	37½c
October	19	64c	35c	66c	44c	83c	38c
October	26	63c	35c	68c	45c	84c	38c
November	2	61c	35c	66c	44c	84c	37½c
November	9	64c	35c	69½c	43c	81c	38½c
November	16	64c	45c	70c	42c	83c	43c
November	23	64c	40c	70c	42c	83½c	40c
November	30	63c	39c	70c	41c	85c	40c

Barley.

The receipts of Barley also show a very large decrease last year as compared with 1854.

The receipts for the past four years by Lake show the following result:

	Bushels.		Bushels.
1852	497,913	1854	313,885
1853	401,098	1855	62,112

Or a decrease last year of 251,773 bushels. But little Barley is sent forward from Western States. There is a good demand at home for all that is grown, and consequently there is none left for shipment. Owing to the very small receipts, all that is offered finds ready purchasers at almost the seller's figures.

There is a large amount of Barley consumed in our city annually, and the following will show from whence we receive our supplies:

	Bushels.
By Lake from Western States	42,112
" " Canada	20,000
By Canal from Interior	81,584
From our own and adjoining counties	20,000
Total	163,696

There have also been shipped by Canal during the past season, 24,390 bushels, which would leave 139,306 bushels for export to Cleveland, to the Western ports and for local consumption.

Owing to the very few sales made in our market, we are unable to present a comparative table of prices. The market opened in the spring at about 80 cents, and ranged from $1.00 to $1.25 and $1.30 during the fall.

Rye.

In the article of Rye, the receipts last year show a very large increase over 1854.

The receipts for the past four years are as follows:

	Bushels.		Bushels.
1852	112,271	1854	177,159
1853	107,152	1855	309,189

Or an increase in favor of 1855 of 132,030 bushels. There were also received by State Line Railroad 19,864 bushels.

The shipments by canal were 221,497 bushels, leaving for consumption in the city about 107,556 bushels. The bulk of the receipts were after harvest, and prices ranged during the season at from 88c to $1.50, closing in the fall at $1.05, the closing quotation of 1854.

Buffalo the Greatest Grain Market in the World.

Buffalo is now universally acknowledged to be the greatest Grain Market on the Continent, not even excepting the city of New York.

It was only eighteen years ago, in 1838, that the first cargo of wheat, or grain of any description, was brought to this city to be sold in this market, by Giles Williams.

The following will show the total receipts of all descriptions of Grain at this port for the past three years by Lake and Railroad:

	Bushels.
1855	20,002,647
1854	18,587,427
1853	11,078,751

| Increase over 1854 | 1,415,220 |
| " " 1853 | 8,923,896 |

The total receipts of Grain in 1855 were	20,002,647
Flour reduced to Wheat	5,019,530
Total Bushels	25,022,177

In connection with the above, we present the following table, showing the average exports of Grain from the principal Grain ports of the world for a series of years, compared with those from Buffalo and Chicago, for the last two years, respectively 1854 and 1855:

	Wheat, Bushels.	Ind. Corn, Bushels.	Oats, Rye & Barley.	Total Bushels.
Odessa	5,600,000		1,440,000	7,040,000
Galetz and Ibrella	2,400,000	5,600,000	320,000	8,320,000
Dantzic	3,080,000		1,328,000	4,408,000
St. Petersburg	all kinds			7,200,000
Archangel	"			9,528,000
Riga	"			4,000,000
Chicago, (1854)	2,644,860	6,337,899	3,419,551	12,902,310
Chicago, (1855)	7,115,250	7,517,625	2,000,938	16,633,813
Buffalo, (1854)	7,209,847	10,109,973	4,966,662	22,286,482
Buffalo, (1855)	13,120,616	8,722,516	3,097,461	25,022,177

In the amount of wheat set down opposite Buffalo and Chicago for the two years, is included Flour, which has been reduced to Wheat at five bushels to the barrel.

These figures, which are reliable, show an excess in favor of Buffalo over Chicago of 8,388,364 bushels, which is more than the total exports of Corn from Chicago, or of Wheat and Flour together.

That the enormous amount of Grain received during the past season at this port has been principally consigned here on Buffalo account, or for sale in this market, we have already shown. We therefore assert, and it is susceptible of proof, that in 1855 the following quantities of produce changed hands in our market, viz:

Flour, bbls	600,000
Wheat, bush	6,500,000
Corn, "	7,500,000
Oats, "	2,000,000
Barley and Rye	300,000

Or about 16,000,000 bushels.

Buffalo, besides being the *"Greatest Grain Port, is the greatest Grain Market in the World."*

Whiskey.

The receipts of whiskey have been gradually declining for several years past, and the passage of the Maine Law, by the Legislature of 1855, has seriously affected our trade, as well as the receipts during the past year. The following will show the receipts for the past four years by Lake:

| 1852 | bbls. 79,306. | 1854 | bbs. 50,287 |
| 1853 | "   66,707. | 1855 | "   36,515 |

or a decrease last year, as compared with 1854, of 14,772 bbls. The State Line Railroad have also brought down 8,697 bbls.

There are two distilleries in the City; that of Clark & Brown and Geo. Truscott, vhich have manufactured during the year ibout 25,000 bbls., consuming nearly 300,-)00 bushels of grain.

As we have already remarked, the passage of the Prohibitory Liquor Law has eriously affected our trade, and the ratification of the Reciprocity Treaty has lso tended to diminish the manufacture of his article in our City. Two firms who ave for a number of years been engaged n this business, and who had their distilleies in the neighborhood of the City, have emoved them to Chippewa, where they re now running about 2,000 bushels of ;rain per day. These firms have always one a large business with Canada, and by emoving to Chippewa they are enabled nder the Reciprocity Treaty to take in heir grain free of duty, and save a duty f eight cents a gallon on the whiskey they nanufacture and sell to Canadian consumrs. The trade between Canada and Clevend has also increased considerably during e past few years. This, added to the igh price of grain which diminished the uantity manufactured in Ohio, is the cause f the large falling off in our receipts.

The shipments by Canal were	759,363	galls.
" " to Canada "	95,116	"
Total,	854,479	

The demand in the market was very acve, through all the season, and the supply as far from meeting the wants of the ade. By the table of comparative prices ' whiskey which we give below, it will be en that it has ruled considerably higher iroughout the greater part of last year ian it did in 1854.

onth D	1853.	1854.	1855.
ly 11	19 to 19¾c	23 to 23¾c	39
ly 18	19½ to 20c	22½ to 23c	39
ly 25	19½ to 20c	23 to 23½c	39
ne 1	19½ to 20c	23½ to 24c	37
ne 8	20 to 21c	25 to 26c	35
ne 15	20 to 21c	24½ to 25c	32
ne 22	20½ to 21c	25 to 26c	35
ne 29	20½ to 21¾c	25½ to 26c	35
ly 6	20¾ to 21c	24 to 24½c	37
ly 13	20¾ to 21c	24½ to 25c	36
ly 20	21 to 21¼c	25 to 25½c	36
ly 27	21½ to 22c	25½ to 26c	37
gust 3	22½ to 23½c	27 to 28c	37
gust 10	23½ to 24c	29 to 30c	37
gust 17	23 to 23¼c	30 to 30¼c	37½
gust 24	23 to 23¼c	31 to 32c	37½
gust 31	22½ to 23c	31 to 32c	37
tember 7	23 to 23¼c	34 to 35c	38
tember 14	24 to 25c	36 to 37c	38
tember 21	23½ to 24c	37 to 37½	38
tember 28	23½ to 24c	36 to 37c	38
ober 5	25¾ to 26c	36½ to 37c	37½
ober 12	26 to 27c	33 to 34c	38
ober 19	28 to 29c	32½ to 33c	38
October 26	27 to 27½c	32 to 32½c	38
November 2	25¾ to 26c	34 to 34½c	37½
November 9	26 to 26½c	34 to 34½c	38
November 16	24¾ to 25c	34 to 35c	36½
November 23	24½ to 24c	38 to 38½c	36½
November 30	24¾ to 25c	38 to 38½c	36½

Provisions.

The receipts of Pork last year show a large falling off as compared with 1854, though an increase over previous years.— The receipts are as follows for the past six years:

1850	bbls. 41,472	1853	bbls. 102,543
1851	" 33,261	1854	" 147,073
1852	" 60,669	1855	" 106,553

A decrease last year of 40,520 bbls.

The decrease last year is to be accounted for in two ways. The facilities which the Rail Roads offer for transporting pork in the hog to the Eastern markets, have been availed of by dealers, as will be seen by the following statement:

Amount of Pork shipped from Chicago for 1854–5, by Lake and Rail Road.

	By Lake.	By Rail Road.	Total.
1854	45,064	23,014	68,078
1855	41,692	35,919	77,611

Number of dressed hogs shipped from Chicago for the same period by Lake and Rail Road:

	Lake.	Rail Road.	Total.
1854	135	12 417	12,552
1855	1,016	55,276	56,292

These tables will show that while there is a slight increase in the shipment of pork for the year, there has been a very large increase in the shipments of dressed hogs as compared with 1854. And in the second place Montreal and other Canadian cities which have hitherto bought largely in our market, have last year made their purchases in western cities. This winter the shipments by Michigan Central and Great Western Railway, will show a still larger increase. From the best information we can obtain about 35,000 hogs have been slaughtered in the City, and 2,515 dressed hogs have been received by Lake, and about 12,179 by the Buffalo and State Line Rail Road, making a total of about 49,694 hogs. Of this number at least 35,000 have been packed in the City for home consumption and for supplying the eastern trade on the line of the Canal and Rail Roads. The amount of Western Pork inspected during the year was about 25,000 bbls. The market during the year has been active and prices were well maintained until the close of Canal navigation, at rates considerably above 1854, as will be seen by the comparative table which we give below.

The receipts of beef for the past six years foot up as follows:

1850 bbls.	74,596	1853 bbls.	69,776
1851 "	70,570	1854 "	56,997
1852 "	76,679	1855 "	98,750

Showing an increase in 1855 over the previous year of 41,953 bbls. For beef there has been a good local demand with some inquiry for the interior, but the bulk of the receipts were sent forward by Rail Road. A very small quantity of beef was packed during the year, and that entirely for home consumption. The quotations throughout the season show a considerable advance on those of 1854.

The receipts of Bacon and Lard as was the case with Pork, show a very large decrease last year. The demand for both articles has been steady, and in the latter a very large business has been done; in part to supply the wants of manufacturers of oil in the City, as well as for the interior of the State, which last year purchased liberally in our market. In Tallow, as in Beef, the receipts show a considerable increase. This article has been principally shipped through, and the sales here have not been large, and only for home wants.

The Dairy products, Butter and Cheese, both show a falling off in the receipts of 1855. In the latter article Buffalo has within a year or two become the centre of a very large and growing trade. In several towns in this County, and in the adjoining Counties of Chautauque, Cattaraugus and Wyoming, the business of making Cheese is a very large one, and the article they produce, known as 'Hamburgh Cheese,' is becoming justly celebrated, and commands a ready market at all times. There are a large number of houses in this City who are engaged in this trade, who have received during the past year nearly two millions and a half pounds, which has been shipped to Canada and We tern States, at prices ranging from 10 to 10½ cts. for good to prime.

Below we present a statement of the weekly average prices for Mess Pork, Mess Beef, and Lard, which shows the course of the market during 1854 and 1855:

		1854.			1855.		
Month	Day	Mess Pork	Mess Beef	Lard	Mess Pork	Mess Beef	Lard
May	4	$13 50	10 50	9¼c	$17 00	13 50	10c
May	11	13 50	10 50	9	17 00	13 50	10
May	18	13 50	10 50	9	17 00	13 50	10
May	25	13 50	10 50	9	17 50	13 25	9¾
June	1	13 00	11 00	9	18 00	13 50	10
June	8	13 00	11 50	9	18 00	13 50	9¾
June	15	13 00	11 50	9	18 00	13 50	10
June	22	13 00	11 50	9	17 75	13 50	10
June	29	13 00	11 50	9	19 00	13 50	10½
July	6	13 00	11 00	9	19 00	13 50	10½
July	13	12 00	11 00	9	18 75	13 50	10½
July	20	12 00	11 00	9	19 00	13 00	11
July	27	12 00	11 00	9	19 25	13 00	11½
August	3	12 00	11 00	9	19 25	13 00	11
August	10	12 00	11 00	9¼	19 25	14 00	11½
August	17	13 00	12 00	9½	19 25	13 50	11½
August	24	13 00	12 00	9½	19 50	13 50	11½
August	31	13 00	12 00	9½	20 50	13 50	12
Sept	7	13 50	12 00	10	21 50	13 50	11¾
Sept	14	14 00	12 00	10¼	21 50	13 00	11¾
Sept	21	14 00	12 00	10¼	22 00	13 00	11¾
Sept	28	14 00	12 00	10¼	22 50	13 00	12
October	5	14 00	12 00	10¼	22 50	13 00	11¾
October	12	14 00	12 00	10½	22 50	13 00	11¾
October	19	13 50	12 00	10½	22 25	13 00	11¾
October	26	13 50	12 00	10½	22 25	13 00	11¾
November	2	13 00	12 00	10½	22 50	13 00	11¾
November	9	13 00	12 00	10	22 00	12 50	11½
November	16	13 00	12 00	10	22 00	12 50	12½
November	23	13 00	12 00	9½	22 00	12 00	12½
November	30	13 00	12 00	9½	21 50	12 00	12½
December	7	13 00	12 00	9¼	20 00	12 00	12½

Live Stock.

Buffalo is admirably located for an ex tensive market for the sale of live stock In the neighborhood of the City there ar extensive pasture farms and cattle yard where large droves which are bro't dow the Lake, or find their way here by Ra Road, are taken to feed and "fill out," pre paratory to their being forwarded to th New York, Cambridge, Brighton, Alban and other Eastern Cattle Markets, whic can be done in the space of a very fe hours. Within a year or two a very larg number of these droves have been sold i these yards to Eastern purchasers; and a attempt was made last year, and which wi undoubtedly prove successful this spring, t establish a regular market here, and hav one or two market days set apart for th purpose. Last year the sales were mad almost every day, and as no report of the was kept, it would be impossible to for any estimate of the number of head sold.

The following will show the comparati number of cattle received by Lake and t State Line Rail Road during the past fo years:

	State Line Rail Road.	Lake.	Total.
1852	4,421	15,926	20,347
1853	13,482	20,466	33,948
1854	43,210	19,047	62,257
1855	51,170	14,112	65,282

Here it will be seen that the total increase in the number received for the past four years is very considerable, and that the increase by Rail Road from year to year is enormous.

We hope that another year will see established a regular Cattle Market in our City; and we know of no place west of Albany where it could be done to better advantage to both drover and purchaser, which will enable us to make a regular weekly report, giving the number sold, price paid, and average quality of those offered.

In live hogs a very large business has been done. A market has been established and several heavy dealers reside in our City. This business is increasing from year to year until it is now one of considerable importance. We learn from a gentleman in the business that over 100,000 hogs changed hands in this market during the the year.

The following will show the number of live hogs brought to this City by the State Line Rail Road and by Lake during the past four years:

	State Line Rail Road.	Lake.	Total.
1852	13,051	171,223	184,274
1853	26,640	114,952	141,952
1854	83,280	74,276	157,556
1855	194,240	54,168	248,406

Probably double the number brought to this City by the State Line Rail Road were left at Dunkirk, to be forwarded to New York by the New York and Erie Rail Road. The establishment of a regular market here would doubtless be the means of bringing a larger number to this point than would otherwise reach New York by the Erie Road.

The number of Sheep brought to this city by the State Line Railroad, and by lake, during the past four years was as follows:

	State Line R. R.	Lake.	Total.
1852	127	16,590	16,717
1853	4,482	23,223	27,705
1854	11,600	19,988	31,588
1855	36,670	26,753	63,423

Here it will be seen that during the past year no less than 377,111 head of Live Stock have been brought to our city, the greater portion of which have remained several days in the yards, or at pasture, on their way to New York, and over half have changed hands in the market, chiefly on speculation.

Salt.

The Salt trade of our city is no considerable one. The large number of beef and pork packing establishments in the west, consume annually a very large quantity of this product of our State, and this supply is obtained through Buffalo and Oswego. The following will show the receipts by Canal for the past four years of domestic salt.

| 1852 | bbls. 221,153 | 1854 | bbls. 221,625 |
| 1853 | bbls. 197,351 | 1855 | bbls. 363,615 |

and of foreign salt during the past two years in pounds:

| 1854 | lbs. 1,049,291 | 1855 | lbs. 240,769 |

The domestic salt finds a ready sale, and is chiefly bought as return freight or for ballast by grain vessels from upper lake ports. It sells at from $1,50 to 1,62½ for fine, and $2,00 to 2,25 for coarse, per bbl.

Lumber.

Buffalo must, within a short time, become a large lumber market, second only to Albany. Our receipts during the year were very large, and the increase from Canada, as compared with 1854, was in value nearly $200,000. Canadian manufacturers last year sent large quantities to this city for sale, and it was purchased by our lumber dealers, of whom there are a great many engaged in the trade. Under the Reciprocity Treaty lumber from Canada is entered as "Timber and Lumber of all kinds, round, hewed and sawed, manufactured in whole or in part," and the value only given; we are therefore unable to give the number of feet. The total value of that imported from Canada in 1855, was $379,522.

The following will show the average receipts for the past four years at this point:

| 1852 | feet 72,337,225 | 1854 | feet 67,407,083 |
| 1853 | feet 89,294,789 | 1855 | feet 73,506,827 |

Last spring a considerable trade sprung up in dressed lumber between this city and Western ports, and several million feet were shipped to Chicago and Milwaukee. We have been unable to obtain any reliable estimate of the amount of Lumber sold in this market during the year.

Wool.

The amount of wool received at this port during the past year, shows a very fair increase. Under the Reciprocity Treaty, the increase in the quantity received from Canada is very large. In 1854, the amount received from Canada was only 3,291 pounds valued at $435, while the receipts in 1855 were 235,237 lbs. and valued at $59,646, an increase of 231,946 lbs, or in value about $59,211.

The following will show the total receipts for the past four years, by lake and railroad.

1852	bls. 45,172	1854	bls 33,671
1853	bls. 45,820	1855	bls 54,682

In addition to this, one million pounds was pulled in this city and vicinity. There are several extensive dealers in the city, one of whom informs us that between 700 and 800,000 lbs. was sold in this market during the year. The greater portion of the receipts have been on account of Eastern dealers, and have gone forward by Railroad. The average price obtained during the season has been for Canada 25c to 30c, and for Western 28c to 40c.

Coal.

The following will show the quantity of Coal received at this point for the past four years. That by Lake was bituminous, and came from Erie and Cleveland, and that received by Canal was anthracite:

	Lake.	Canal.	Total.
1852	Tons 34,665	22,894	57,559
1853	Tons 38,188	23,313	61,501
1854	Tons 57,634	35,314	92,948
1855	Tons 60,123	43,040	103,163

There were also brought to this city by railroad about 2,500 tons.

Of the bituminous Coal, 10,388 tons were shipped east by Canal, and of the anthracite about 40,000 tons were shipped to western states and Canada. This would leave for city consumption and for supplying our Steamers, about 55,275 tons.

The bituminous Coal has brought in the market by the cargo, $4,50a5 per ton; and at retail $5,50a6. The anthracite has sold for $6,50 to $8,50 for Lackawanna, Scranton, Blosburg, Schuylkill and Lehigh.

Lake Imports for 1855.

The following table will show the quantity and value of the principal articles received by Lake at this port during the season of 1855:

Articles.		Quantity.	Value.
Flour	bbls.	937,223	$7,966,395
Corn Meal	bbls.	892	4,460
Rye Flour	bbls.	1,016	9,096
Pork	bbls.	106,553	1,705,848
Beef	bbls.	98,750	1,185,000
Ashes	bbls.	4,427	132,810
Whiskey	bbls.	36,515	547,725
Seeds	bbls.	22,560	225,600
Eggs	bbls.	5,600	67,200
Fish	bbls.	7,241	50,687
Cranberries	bbls.	237	2,844
Oil	bbls.	4,887	146,610
Tongues	bbls.	620	19,600
Nuts	bbls.	376	1,980
Beans	bbls.	162	810
Hides	No.	92,564	370,256
Leather	Rolls.	2,740	68,500
Broom Corn	Bls.	10,116	121,392
Buffalo Robes	Bls.	536	40,200
Copper	bbls.	356	213,600
Copper	Tons.	215	21,500
Coal	Tons.	60,123	300,615
Iron (Pig)	Tons.	4,020	160,800
Iron	Bars.	3,115	9,345
Iron	bdls.	1,513	7,565
Iron scraps	bbls.	420	2,520
Iron blooms		982	3,948
Lead	pigs.	66,118	330,590
Wheat	bu.	8,076,821	14,538,277
Corn	bu.	8,722,516	7,239,688
Oats	bu.	2,683,123	1,341,561
Barley	bu.	62,112	77,642
Rye	bu.	309,189	304,107
Butter	lbs.	1,996,574	399,314
Cheese	lbs.	756,830	90,819
Lard	lbs.	10,567,823	1,056,782
Tallow	lbs.	1,862,179	186,217
Bacon	lbs.	10,876,530	1,087,653
Grease	lbs.	755,900	60,472
Tobacco	hhds.	596	44,700
Tobacco	boxes.	3,572	125,020
Tobacco	bbls.	156	3,120
Wool	bls.	47,864	2,871,840
Flax	bls.	1,232	18,480
Hemp	bls.	2,162	29,050
Cotton	bls.	238	11,900
Pelts	bls.	4,813	120,325
Furs	pkgs.	1,160	174,000
Lumber	ft.	73,506,827	1,470,136
Staves	No.	16,915,221	845,761
Shingles	No.	1,821,347	72,853
Lath	No.	396,125	11,883
Cedar Posts	No.	8,561	2,568
Feathers	Sacks.	426	4,260
Horses	No.	386	38,600
Cattle	No.	14,112	1,128,960
Sheep	No.	26,753	80,259
Hogs (Live)	No.	54,168	650,010
Hogs (Dressed)	No.	2,515	37,725
Rags	bags.	1,824	9,120
Paper	bdls.	8,600	86,000
Hair	pkgs.	518	3,108
Wax	bbls.	220	6,600
Glue	bbls.	197	2,364
Starch	bbls.	630	6,300
Starch	boxes.	820	2,050
Soap	boxes.	730	2,920
Candles	boxes.	1,587	12,696
Skins (Deer)	bdls.	1,865	93,250
Skins (Calf)	bdls.	971	971
Sugar	hhds.	27	2,700
Railroad Ties	No.	32,723	8,180
Brick	No.	133,000	1,596
Plaster	bbls.	176	528
Oil Cake	bags & bbls.	15,896	47,688
Oil Cake	Tons.	998	19,960
Paint	Kegs.	220	1,760
Nails	Kegs.	1,033	5,165
Saleratus	bbls.	72	1,440
Saleratus	boxes.	220	1,320
Dried fruit	bbls.	1,561	15,610
Peas	bags.	830	830
Glass Ware	csks.	1,622	16,220
Glass Ware	boxes.	6,531	25,124
Grindstones	Tons.	1,722	34,440
Grindstones	No.	4,336	13,008
Shorts	bags.	10,331	8,265
Hops	bls.	130	9,750
Cement	bbls.	61	91
Rope	coils.	230	4,600
Potatoes	bu.	23,000	11,500
Ship Knees	No.	4,160	41,600
Oars	No.	8,236	2,059

TRADE AND COMMERCE OF

Washbowls		Nests	1,326	6,630
Sundries		pkgs		2,000,000

Total Value	$50,346,819
Total Value in 1854	42,030,931
Increase in favor of 1855	$8,315,888

The following table shows the principal articles landed at this port, from the opening to the close of navigation, for four seasons:

	1852.	1853.	1854.	1855.
Flour...bbls	1,299,513	983,837	739,811	937,223
Pork	60,669	102,548	147,073	106,553
Beef	76,679	69,776	56,997	98,750
Whiskey	79,306	66,707	50,287	36,515
Corn Meal	5,099	311	2,540	892
Seed	31,559	37,018	20,185	22,560
Eggs	7,686	11,000	8,012	5,600
Fish	6,814	7,773	11,752	7,241
Oil	7,577	7,965	9,425	4,887
Ashes..cks	14,522	11,558	7,553	4,427
Wheat..bu	5,549,778	5,424,043	3,510,792	8,076,821
Corn	5,136,746	3,665,793	10,109,973	8,722,516
Oats	2,596,231	1,480,655	4,475,618	2,683,123
Rye	112,271	107,152	177,159	309,189
Barley	497,913	401,098	313,885	62,112
Butter..lbs	3,989,917	6,589,784	3,783,526	1,996,574
Cheese		5,377,800	1,464,200	756,830
Lard	7,164,672	8,185,300	13,575,662	10,567,823
Tallow	1,014,686	762,810	576,450	1,862,879
Bacon	9,696,590	23,075,645	20,488,400	10,876,530
Wool, bales	45,172	45,820	33,671	47,864
Hemp	3,597	1,977	4,222	1,162
Flax	789	520	635	1,232
Broom Corn	5,420	4,963	5,783	10,116
Buff Robes	80	631	65	536
Feathers	2,285	1,556	1,209	426
Pelts	3,296	5,288	4,550	4,813
Furs, pkgs	2,909	1,095	1,664	1,160
Leather	7,155	7,991	4,226	2,740
Hides...No	95,452	98,008	68,427	92,564
Copper, ton	439	1,068	1,760	215
Iron	4,848	4,731	4,304	4,020
Coal	34,665	38,188	57,634	60,123
Lead, pigs	31,916	36,004	44,978	66,118
Tobacco, hd	6,620	2,038	2,849	596
Tobacco, bx	7,099	5,030	6,659	3,576
Lumber, ft	72,337,225	89,294,789	67,407,083	73,506,827
Shingles, M	13,532,000	3,542,642	1,658,000	1,821,347
Lath	1,500,000	2,058,920	191,000	396,125
Staves, No	12,998,614	9,215,240	16,437,015	16,915,221
Horses	1,643	1,533	743	386
Cattle	15,926	20,466	19,047	14,112
Sheep	16,590	23,223	19,988	26,753
Live Hogs	171,223	114,952	74,276	54,168

The total value of the Imports by Lake for the year 1854, as appears by our figures is $50,346,819, or an increase as compared with 1854 of $8,315,888. These tables as has been the case for the past three years, we have been compelled to make up from our daily, weekly and monthly statements of Imports by Lake. Prior to that period, they were furnished the press by the Custom House Clerks, but since then they have not been required by the Department at Washington to make them out. We are satisfied however that they are far more correct than any tables which could be made out from the Custom House records.

The above comparative table will show the increase during the past year in the imports of wheat to be over 4,500,000 bushels. Flour shows an increase in favor of the past year of $197,412 bbls. Beef an increase of 41,753 bbls, and Rye, Wool, Iron, Coal, and Lumber, show a handsome increase. While in Pork there is a decrease of 40,520 bbls. Whiskey 13,772 barrels Corn of 1,287,457 bushels; Oats of 1,792,495 bushels; Barley of 251,773 bushels and Butter, Cheese, Lard, and Bacon, show a large falling off. Notwithstanding the large decrease on several articles, our imports taken as a whole, show a very large and gratifying increase over previous years. That the decrease in our receipts at this port in a large number of articles is not the result of their division to other channels and routes in seeking a market is too obvious to be denied, and will easily be seen by examining the receipts at other receiving ports, with perhaps the exception of the article of pork and the products of the hog. Montreal and other Canadian cities which have heretofore purchased largely in this market have, during the past year obtained the greater portion of their supplies direct from the west.

The increase in the value of our Imports is not owing as was the case a year ago, to the advance in prices of nearly all descriptions of produce, but to the increase in quantity of several of the more valuable products.

The amount of specie on deposit in the Custom House in this city on the 24th December, 1855, and subject to draft was only $3,486 67. Buffalo is a United State's Depository for several collection districts, and the fact of large drafts for refunded duties under the Reciprocity Treaty, as well as drafts for the pay of Government offices and others being paid here, with but a small amount of duties collected keeps the amount on deposit in this city very low.

The amount paid out by the collector of this district during the past year for the relief of destitute and disabled or sick seamen, was $4,425 33, an increase over the previous year of $189 78; and the amount collected in this district during the year for that fund was $2.307 81—leaving a deficit of $2,117 52, which is made up by appropriation by the General Government. The amount collected in the District is by a tax on seamen of twenty-five cents per month ich is retained from their wages, and ich is paid into the Custom Hou e by ssel owners every year when they re- w their licenses. The number of seamen ιο have been admitted into the hospital ιring the year was 210, and the aggregate mber of days of relief furnished was 7665. 3 there is no Marine Hospital in the city e Government have a contract with the e Trustees of the Hospital of the Sisters of arity, to which place those in need of re- f are sent, and are there attended by a edical man appointed by the collector of e port.

The table which we give below shows an crease for the year in the total number of rivals and departures of 259, while it ows a decrease in the tonnage of 665,051 ns. This discrepency is to be accounted r from the fact that the line of large pas- nger steamers running between this city id Sandusky in 1854, (we refer to the St. wrence and Mississippi,) were laid up all st season, and also the withdrawal of se- ral large passenger steamers which ran tween this port and Chicago, as well as the fact that the Cleveland and Southern ichigan lines of Steamers did not com- ence running last spring until much later the season than was their usual custom, d to their being laid up early in the fall.) this cause may be assigned the apparent crease in the amount of tonnage last year compared with 1854. Taking these facts to consideration, it will be seen that there s been a handsome increase in freight nnage over any other year.

The following table shows the entrances d clearances at this port of Foreign and merican vessels, together with their ton- ige and crews during the year 1855:

Arrived.	No.	Tons.	Men.
nerican Vessels from			
Foreign Ports	318	122,958 91	3,512
reign do do	730	68,549 33	5,870
Total	1048	191,508 29	9,382
Cleared.			
nerican Vessels to			
Foreign Ports	353	122,256 91	3,735
reign do do	666	61,133 30	5,516
Total	1,019	183,390 26	9,251
Coasting Trade.			
wards	3,595	1,517,265 88	49,702
itwards	3,569	1,438,069 23	39,668
Total	7,164	2,955,335 16	89,370

Grand Total			
1855	9,231	3,360,233 71	111,515
1854	8,972	3,995,284 19	120,838
1853	8,298	3,252,978 26	128,112
1852	9,441	3,092,247 73	127,491
1851	9,050	3,087,533 80	120,542
1850	8,444	2,713,700 86	125,672

Ship Building.

In compiling our annual statement of the business done in ship building at this port, the amount of vessel tonnage turned out during the past year, together with what is now on the stocks, exhibit a very considerable increase in this branch of in- dustry over the previous year.

Buffalo is pre-eminently a ship building port, and her mechanics have turned out some of the most magnificent floating pal- aces belonging to this country. The sail vessels also, in point of model, rig and fin- ish, will compare favorably with those of New York, or any other seaport. Ship building is just now, and has been, since early last spring, in a very prosperous con- dition. During the winter of 1854-5, ow- ing to the tightness of the money market, and the general depression that pervaded all branches of business, but little activity was to be seen in any of our ship-yards, but with the opening of navigation and the commencement of business in the early part of the season, more confidence was apparent on all hands, and, with the prospect of an abundant harvest and high freights on the Lakes, a large number of new vessels were contracted for, to be ready for the fall trade. The harvest last fall having proved abun- dant, and the prospects of a large increase in the carrying trade of the lakes next spring, has stimulated the activity of our ship builders this winter to the highest de- gree, as will be seen by the tables which follow.

Below we present a list of the vessels that have been built at this port during the past summer, as well as those now on the stocks and to be launched in the spring. From the first table it will be seen that the aggregate tonnage turned out during the year 1855 was less than in 1854, while the number of vessels shows an increase. In 1854 two large passenger steamers were constructed, having an aggregate tonnage of nearly 4000 tons. Our lakes are now well supplied with this class of vessels, and it will only be when a new one is wanted to replace one that may be condemned—as, for instance, the one now building to take the place of the Empire State in the Southern Michigan Line—that these large steamers will be built. There has, therefore, been a large increase in the amount of freight tonnage turned out last year. During the past year, which has been one of the most disastrous to our lake marine ever known, it will be seen that Buffalo has sustained her share in the losses. The amount of tonnage belonging to this District which has gone out of existence during the year, is more than made up by the new tonnage built at this port and enrolled in this District, and by that built in other Districts for residents of this city.

During the past year the demand for vessels has so increased that one firm, who have hitherto been engaged in canal boat building, have extended their operations, and have built during the year several tugs, and have now two propellers, two tugs and three schooners on the stocks in their yard. They are also building several canal boats. We refer to Messrs. Van Slyke, Notter & Co.

Three new yards have also commenced operations during the year, and are now in full blast. The yards belong to George Hardison, B. B. Jones and Seth C. Jones. The two former are located on the creek above the depot of the Buffalo and New York City Railroad, and the latter is on the Erie Basin.

As we have already remarked, this branch of trade is extensively carried on in our city, and the demand for new vessels has been unusually active during the past summer and present winter. As a natural consequence, lumber and other materials have considerably advanced in price, but the supply is hardly equal to the demand. Labor also is high, but nearly 2,000 men have obtained constant employment during the winter months, and when we come to add in their families, and others dependant on these men for their support, it will be seen that a very large number of persons are reaping the benefits of the unusual activity in our ship-yards.

The following is a list of the steamers, propellers, and sail vessels, by whom built, with their tonnage and value at this port during the year 1855:

Steamer	Builder	Tons
Union	Bidwell & Banta	80
Propellers		
Chicago	Bidwell & Banta	770
Relief	Van Slyke, Notter & Co.	362
Mary Bell	" " "	75
	" " "	75
Rescue	Bidwell & Banta	285
Dime	" "	47
Total of Steam		1,694
Sail Vessels.		
Barque		
John Sweeney	F. N. Jones	406
Schooners		
Antelope	O'Conner	347
Genoa	"	197
Convoy	"	360
C. L. Abell	Hardison	70
Lookout	"	313
Curtis Mann	"	396
Golden Harvest	B. B. Jones	376
Collingwood	"	376
Eliza Logan	"	369
Grapeshot	"	369
Perseverance	F. N. Jones	306
Enterprize	"	306
Bay State	"	350
J. F. Tracey	"	200
Rainbow	"	350
Contest	"	360
Atlair	"	412
Yankee Blade	"	350
Theodore Parker	Bidwell & Banta	309
John P. Hale	" "	309
Geritt Smith	" "	309
Wings of the Wind.	" "	370
Mary Smith	" "	370
L. B. Shepard	Laveyea	290
Mozelle	"	331
Sail Tonnage		8,481
Steam "		1,694
		10,175
Repairs, &c		
		$72

As we have already stated, there i[s] very large amount of new tonnage on stocks, to be launched in season for spring business, and commenced in the of 1855.

At Bidwell & Banta's yard there is the stocks a first class steamer of nea[r] 2000 tons burthen, and of the following mensions: Length, 330 feet; Breadth Beam 40 feet, and Depth of hold 14 f[eet] This steamer is to receive the engine of steamer Empire State, and will run in [the] Southern Michigan line. When comple[te] she will cost about $200,000.

They are building a propeller for P. Sternberg & Co., to run in the West[ern] Transportation Company's line, to c[ost] about $50,000, and of the following dime[n] sions: Length, 198 feet; Breadth of Bea[m] 31 feet 4 inches, and Depth of Hold feet 10 inches.

One propeller for A. T. Spencer & C[o.] of Chicago, to run in the Lake Super[ior]

; to cost about $40,000, and of the
...ving dimensions: Length, 197 feet,
...lth 30 feet, and Depth of Hold 11

...ie propeller for Capt. Robert Mont-
...ry, of this city, to cost $45,000 and to
...ure in length 197 feet, breadth 30 feet,
...depth of hold 12 feet.

...iey are also building a propeller for
...ard & Co., and for their own account,
...h will be worth about $45,000, and of
...following dimensions: Length, 176
... beam 33 feet and depth 12½ feet.

...lso, a steam tug of about 200 tons bur-
..., to cost $18,000, and which will be
...t 100 feet in length, 20 feet beam and
...t hold. This vessel they are building
...eculation.

...is firm have also on the stocks some
...schooners for Bruce & Co., of Chicago.
...out 350 tons burthen each, and to cost
...000 each. They will be about 138 feet
...ngth, 26 feet beam, and 10½ feet hold,
...will all be out next spring or early in
...summer.

...iey are also about contracting to build
...or three more vessels for an Oswego
...e. This firm have now on the stocks,
...ted above:

	Tons.	Value.
...eamer	2,000	$200,000
...ropellers	2,800	181,000
...ig	200	18,000
...hooners	1,750	85,000
	6,750	$484,000

...t F. N. Jones' yard there are three
...ls on the stocks of about 300 tons
... for E. K. Bruce and others, and to cost
...t $15,500 each.

...lso, three schooners for Niles & Kinne,
...easure about 280 tons, and to cost about
...000 each.

...ne schooner for Alexander Miller, of
...t 356 tons, and to cost $17,000, and
... for Capt. Hart and Capt. Pratt, to
...sure 370 tons, and to cost $19,000.
...se vessels are all first class, and will be
...n the spring. There are at this yard,
...ie stocks, as noted above, 8 schooners,
...inting to 2,466 tons, and valued at
...,500.

...t B. B. Jones' yard there are on the
...s one propeller for P. L. Sternberg &
... and to run in the Western Transpor-
...n Co.'s Line, of about 800 tons burthen
and of the following dimensions: 200 feet in length, 32 feet beam, and 13 feet depth of hold, and to cost about $50,000.

Mr. Jones is also building three schooners of about 370 tons burthen, to cost about $18,000 each, for Mixer & Bro.

And one for Alexander Miller, of about 375 tons, and to cost about $18,000. At this yard, as stated above, there is one Propeller, of 800 tons, valued at $50,000, and four schooners, of 1,480 tons, making a total of 2,280 tons, valued at $118,000.

At E. K. Bruce's yard there are on the stocks three schooners for himself and Capt. Dimick, one to measure about 360 tons, and to cost $17,000, one about 230 tons, to cost $10,000, and another of about 200 tons, to cost $8,000. At this yard there are in process of construction three schooners, measuring 890 tons and valued at $35,000.

At Geo. Hardison's yard there are on the stocks one propeller, of about 745 tons burthen, for C. Hitchcock & Co., and to measure 190 feet in length, 33 feet breadth of beam, and 12 feet 6 inches depth of hold, and to cost $45,000.

One schooner for Joseph Kellogg, of Erie, to be about 340 tons burthen and to cost $15,500. Total at this yard on the stocks:

	Tons.	Value.
1 Propeller	745	$45,000
1 Schooner	340	15,500
Total	1,085	$60,500

At S. C. Jones' yard there are three schooners on the stocks, which will rate from 375 to 400 tons each, and will cost from 18 to 20,000 dollars, which will make at this yard 3 schooners, of 1,175 tons burthen and valued at $58,000.

At Van Slyke, Notter & Co's yard there are now on the stocks one propeller, of about 500 tons burthen, for W. D. Walbridge, and to run in the American Transportation Company's line; to cost $30,000.

One propeller for Charles Bancroft, of Detroit, to be about 750 tons burthen, and to cost about $45,000. Its dimensions are: Length 175 feet, breadth 31 feet and depth of hold 12 feet.

One tug of about 550 tons for the Chicago Mutual Insurance Company, and to cost about $25,000.

One tug for Mr. Bell of about 125 tons; to cost $5,000.

One schooner of 400 tons for Taylor & Jewitt; to cost $18,000.

One of about 300 tons for Walter Joy; to cost about $9,000.

The amount of tonnage now on the stocks at this yard foots up as follows:

	Tons.	Value.
2 Propellers	1,250	$75,000
2 Tugs	675	30,000
2 Schooners	700	27,000
Total	1,875	132,000

At Laveyea's yard two schooners were built during the past year for Morse & Johnson.

At present there is nothing doing in this yard, and the proprietor is absent at the West. We understand that he will probably build one schooner during the spring.

RECAPITULATION.

The following will show the number of vessels at the different yards now on the stocks, as noted above, with their tonnage and value:

Yard.	No.	Class.	Tons.	Value.
Bidwell & Banta	1	Steamer	2,000	200,000
"	4	Propellers	2,800	180,000
"	1	Tug	200	18,000
"	5	Schooners	1,750	85,000
F. N. Jones	8	Schooners	2,466	127,000
B. B. Jones	1	Propeller	800	50,000
"		4 Schooners	1,480	68,000
E. K. Bruce	3	Schooners	890	35,000
George Hardison	1	Propeller	745	45,000
"	1	Schooner	340	15,500
S. C. Jones	3	Schooners	1,175	58,000
Van Slyke, Notter & Co	2	Propellers	1,250	75,000
Van Slyke, Notter & Co	2	Tugs	675	30,000
Van Slyke, Notter & Co	2	Schooners	700	27,000
Total	38		17,271	1,013,500

The same table, in another form, would sum up thus:

1 Steamer of	2,000 tons,	worth	200,000
8 Propellers	5,595 "	"	350,000
3 Tugs of	875 "	"	48,000
26 Schooners	8,801 "	"	415,500
38	17,271		1,013,500

In addition to the above, the American Transportation Company are building at Milwaukee a propeller of about 500 tons to take the place of the Alleghany, wrecked last fall.

At Cleveland, Luther Mosses is building a propeller for Messrs. Wm. Foot, Samuel Morgan and Capt. Pheatt, of this city, to measure about 775 tons, and to be ready for the spring trade. Her dimensions are 200 feet in length, 13 feet hold and beam; she will cost $50,000.

R. Calkins, of Cleveland, is buil[ding a] schooner of 350 tons burthen for [Alexan]der Miller, of this city.

Capt. Howard is also building, a[Con]neaut, for E. K. Bruce, of this [city, a] schooner of about 450 tons, and [to cost] about $19,000.

Mr. Smith is building, at Saginaw [a fore] and aft schooner of 300 tons, and ab[out the] dimensions of the schooner Quickst[ep for] J. R. Bentley & Co., of this city.

The above are the only vessels t[hat we] have heard of, building at other lak[e ports] for parties in this city, but there are [doubt]less several more.

The following table will show the [name,] tonnage and value of new vessels [that] have been built during the year 185[5 and] added to the tonnage of this District[:]

Class.	Name.	Tonage
Steamer	Union	80
Propeller	Chicago	758
Propeller	Potomac	814
Propeller	T. U. Bradbury	556
Propeller	Relief	362
Propeller	Rescue	285
Tug	Dime	47
Tug	May Bell	75
Tug	O. N. Chapin	47
Tug	G. O. Vail	52
Tug		75
	Steam	3140
Brig	Canopus	386
Barque	John Sweeny	406
Schooner	Genoa	197
Schooner	Antelope	327
Schooner	Convoy	360
Schooner	C. L. Abell	70
Schooner	Lookout	313
Schooner	Curtis Mann	396
Schooner	Golden Harvest	376
Schooner	Collingwood	376
Schooner	Eliza Logan	369
Schooner	Grapeshot	369
Schooner	Perseverance	306
Schooner	Enterprise	306
Schooner	Bay State	350
Schooner	J. F. Tracy	200
Schooner	Rainbow	350
Schooner	Contest	360
Schooner	Altair	412
Schooner	Yankee Blade	350
Schooner	L. B. Shepard	290
Schooner	Mozelle	336
Schooner	Sea Star	120
Sail		7325
Steam		3140
Total		10,465

There have also been added to thi[s Dis]trict, by purchase from other Lake [Dis]tricts, so far as we have been able to [ascer]tain, two barques, two brigs and five s[choo]ners, having an aggregate tonnage of [____] tons, and valued at $75,000.

ral vessels have also been sold out of District, whose aggregate tonnage about balance the amount of tonnought and brought into this District

following will show the names, tonnd value of vessels belonging to the of Buffalo Creek, which have been l and become a total loss during the 55:

	Tons.	Value.
Oregon	312	8,000
Alleghany	468	8,000
Charter Oak	184	5,000
arora	253	6,000
ina	160	2,500
Mansfield	213	7,000
Ivanhoe	237	7,000
	1,827	43,500
ge to vessels still in existence		146,635
otal damage to Marine of this District		199,135

e were also vessels lost, enrolled in Districts, in which residents of our re part owners.

854 this District lost 4,908 tons by and during the past year the total s only 1827 tons, showing a decrease l tons in favor of the past year.— mage to the marine of this District r was not one-third what it was in while the damage to the marine of ole Lakes shows an excess in 1855, pared with 1854, of $633,704.

following statement will show the mber of different class of vessels ennn the District of Buffalo Creek on st December, 1855, with their aggtonnage and valuation:

Class.	Tons.	Value.
Steamers	18,997	$1,698,000
Propellers	21,660	995,000
Barques	3,579	110,000
Brigs	8,092	211,500
Schooners	22,638	708,000
	74,966	$3,722,500
	64,942	3,235,200
	10,024	487,300

Secretary of the Treasury, in his re- "Commerce and Navigation" for puts down the tonnage of Buffalo t 76,952 55-95 tons. This is, howcorrect, and the same may be said of ther Lake Districts, as stated in that

Vessels which have been out of exfor years, but the fact not having fficially reported at the Custom or their enrollments cancelled, are l in the report of the Secretary of asury. In our figures we have struck out all such, and our table, as given above, is, we believe, as near correct as it is possible to make it.

Trade with Canada.

The Reciprocity Treaty, which was ratified by the Canadian and other Provincial Governments early in the spring of 1855, and which went into operation about the middle of March last, has wrought a wonderful change in the trade between this port and Canada. The effects which the friends of that Treaty predicted, are fully realized in the increased and constantly increasing commercial intercourse between this country and the Provinces. That Treaty has scarcely been in operation nine months, and already it is strenuously urged on both sides of the line that the principle of Reciprocity should be extended to manufactures, shipping and the coasting trade, while some go so far as to demand free and unrestricted trade between Canada and the United States. We do not deem this a proper time to discuss the merits of the question, reserving that for a future occasion, when we shall be in possession of statistics of the Canadian trade of other ports on the lakes.

This being the first year under the operation of this Treaty, we have deemed it a matter of considerable importance to make our tables of the trade between our port and Canada as complete as possible. This we believe we have succeeded in doing, after a vast amount of labor in compiling and arranging the statements which follow. The embarrassments which the Buffalo, Brantford and Goderich Railroad have had to encounter during the past year, and which are referred to more fully under the head of "Railroads," thereby interrupting the traffic on this line between this city and its intersection with the Great Western Railway at Paris, has seriously affected the trade between that portion of the province, through which the road runs, and our city. It has caused a very large diversion of the trade from this road to the Niagara Falls Road and the Suspension Bridge. We know of one firm who have shipped high wines from this city to Canada, via the Suspension Bridge, during the past season, on which duties to the amount of over $500 have been paid. It will therefore be seen that our tables of exports, as obtained from the Custom House, do not by any means show our entire export trade, but merely the direct trade with the ports along the Canadian shore.

The tables which we give below will show that the Imports of dutiable goods, produce, merchandize, &c., before the operation of the Reciprocity Treaty were	$69,912 66
That the Imports of free goods, produce, merchandize, &c., under the Reciprocity Treaty, during the year were	1,987,957 57
That the Imports of free goods and merchandize under the tariff of 1846 were	66,081 02
And the Imports of dutiable goods under the Reciprocity Treaty were	9,253 99
Making a total of Canadian Imports for 1855 of	$2,131,205 24

In 1854 the Imports of foreign produce, merchandize and goods were	$442,087 26
Do. do. in bond for transportation	448,104 00
Do. do. of free goods	132,671 00
Total Imports in 1854	$1,022,862 26
" " in 1855	2,131,205 24
Increase in favor of 1855	$1,108,342 98

Under the Reciprocity Treaty a new system of keeping the accounts of the Import and Export trade has been adopted, which renders it very difficult to make exact comparisons of the trade of different years. Hitherto flour, rye flour, corn meal, buckwheat flour and shorts were kept separately; now they are all included under the head of "Breadstuffs," and are estimated by cwt. instead of bbls. or bags, and wheat, corn, rye, oats and barley come under the head of "Grain of all kinds." This classification is much to be regretted, and we trust the old system will again be resumed.

It will be seen that the amount of flour received prior to the Reciprocity Treaty was 2,328 bbls., while of buckwheat flour, corn meal and shorts, the total was 3,752 lbs., or about 20 bbls. After the Reciprocity Treaty, the receipts of flour and breadstuffs was 116,806 cwt., which is equal to 66,746 bbls., and after deducting the same proportion from this amount as we have above, it would leave fully 65,000 bbls. flour and 1,746 of the other descriptions. We are also told by the Clerk in the Custom House who has charge of this department, that nearly the whole amount entered as flour and breadstuffs, was flour. We therefore incline to the belief that our estimate is correct.

	Bbls.
The Imports of flour in 1854 was	34,879
" " " " 1855 "	67,328
Increase in 1855	32,449

Again, the total receipts of grain of all descriptions were 546,242 bushels afte[r] Reciprocity Treaty, and before it went [into] operation the receipts were: wheat, [bush.] 23,416; barley, bush., 3,085; corn [bush.], which would therefore make [the] average proportion of the former amou[nt to] be—of wheat 476,242 bushels, and o[f] other descriptions of grain at 70,000. [This] would give the total receipts of wheat [for] the year 1855 at about 500,000 bus[hels]. In 1854 the receipts were 154,145 bus[hels]. Increase in 1855, 345,855.

In addition to flour and grain, it wi[ll be] seen that there is a very large increas[e in] the value of lumber and wool importe[d in] 1855, as compared with 1854.

The value of the lumber imported in 1855 was	$379,[?]
" " " " 1854 "	199,[?]
Increase in 1855	$180,[?]
The value of the wool imported in 1855 was	59,[?]
" " " " 1854 "	[?]
Increase in 1855	59,[?]

These are the principal articles whic[h we] receive from Canada, and it will be [seen] that under the Reciprocity Treaty they show a very handsome increase. Ve[geta]bles to the amount of $24,306 75 [have] also been imported during the year.

The exports of domestic and for[eign] produce, manufactures and merchan[dize] show a considerable decrease from 185[4.]

The Exports of domestic produce, &c., in 1855 were	8[?]
The Exports of foreign produce, &c., in 1855 were	8[?]
Total in 1855	9[?]
" 1854	1,1[?]
Decrease in 1855	2[?]
The total Canadian trade in 1855 was	$3,066,3[?]
" " " 1854 "	2,175,0[?]
Increase in 1855	$891,3[?]
The amount of duties collected in 1855 was	$29,2[?]
In 1854	99,6[?]
Decrease in 1855	$70,3[?]

The greater portion of the above am[ount] of duties was collected before the opera[tion] of the Reciprocity Treaty, and was co[nse]quently refunded. The amount of du[ties] collected on foreign merchandise com[ing] through in bond was $17,220 22.

The amount of duties refunded at the [U.] S. Depository in this city, under the Tre[aty] was nearly $50,000.

Abstract of dutiable goods and m[er]chandise imported into the District of [?]

THE CITY OF BUFFALO.

...reek from the 1st of January, 1855, ... 8th of March, when the Reciprocity ...y went into full force and effect, in ...ican vessels:

...es.	Quantity.	Value.	Duties.
...bls	2,328	$17,276 10	$3,455 20
...eat Flour, lbs	180	6 46	1 29
...eal, lbs	70	1 08	22
...lbs	3,502	26 89	5 38
...bush	20,665	32,069 20	6,418 82
"	3,004	2,888 34	577 68
"	25	8 59	1 72
s "	96	51 00	15 30
No	2	184 50	36 90
"	22	209 09	41 82
"	2	19 78	3 96
...bls	32	619 02	123 81
...lbs	28	3 59	1 08
...d Bedding	1	10 25	3 08
No	1	2 56	77
...ron, lbs	6,800	69 70	20 91
...per, "	2,099	241 73	12 03
...ns		172 25	17 22
Pine Boards and ..., feet	85,785	441 00	88 22
...nber, feet	370	22 75	4 55
...ocks, No	94	4 45	1 34
...tured Pine Lum- ...ber	2,000	20 50	6 15
...ots, No	48	18 45	5 53
...les and Skins		709 11	132 20
...s	850	217 81	65 34
...ills	40	7 18	2 15
...y and Glass Ware		8,114 49	2,434 31
...s	3,200	65 60	3 28
otal		$63,481 47	$13,475 34

...tement of dutiable goods and mer-...ise imported into the District of Buf-...reek from the 1st of January, 1855, ...8th of March, when the Reciprocity ...y went into full force and effect, in ...n vessels:

...es.	Quantity.	Value.	Duties.
...bu	2,751	4,030 52	806 11
...bu	81	83 03	16 60
...les and Skins, No	1,046	264 08	52 82
...s, Galls	10	10 25	3 08
...bbls	2	3 84	77
...bs	82½	15 38	3 08
...s	400	20 50	4 10
...No	1	3 59	72
...l in Foreign Vessels		4,431 19	887 28
" American "		63,481 47	13,475 34
Grand Total		$67,912 66	$14,362 62

...tement of produce and goods im-...into the District of Buffalo Creek ...are free under the Reciprocity Treaty ...he time that Treaty went into full ...on the 8th of March, to the 31st De-...r, 1855, in American vessels:

...s.	Quantity.	Value.
...all kinds, bu	186,630½	$322,521 73
...d Breadstuffs, cwt	61,980	291,316 02
..., (not breeding) No	1,427	15,713 84
...lants, &c		35 00
...es, bbls	30,413	21,992 23
...No	1,045	213 18
...indred	843	873 50
...d Skins, (undressed) No	556	1,615 95
...ndressed) No	340	140 00
...bs	12,535½	2,030 79
...bs	993	96 70

Timber and Lumber of all kinds		66,713 06
Pelts, No	11,533	5,894 66
Wool, lbs	91,202	22,873 28
Rags, lbs	17,749	414 51
Fresh, Smoked and Salted Meat, lbs	8,948	747 00
Fruit, (dried) bu	1	1 00
Fruit, (undried) bu	281	109 00
Cheese, lbs	120	12 00
Ashes, lbs	7,400	302 00
Horns, No	4,100	67 00
Fire Wood, cords	11	26 00
Total in American Vessels		$753,708 45

Statement of produce and goods imported into the District of Buffalo Creek which are free of duty under the Reciprocity Treaty, from the time that Treaty went into full force, on the 8th of March, to the 31st December, 1855, in foreign vessels:

Articles.	Quantity	Value
Grain of all kinds bu	359,612	$631,758,89
Flour and Breadstuffs cwt	54,826	232,541,98
Animals not for breed No	424	5,166,75
Seeds plants &c		512
Vegitables bu	3,235½	2,314,52
Fish lbs	1,300	40,29
Eggs hundred	18	16,20
Hides and skins undressed No	587	1,218,88
Furs undressed No	9,994	1,115,35
Butter lbs	1,908	320,86
Horns No	4,000	143,03
Ashes lbs	16,600	849,74
Timber and Lumber of all kinds		312,307,04
Pelts No	20,128	9,227,19
Wool lbs	143,185	36,654,89
Rags lbs	14,527	346,39
Fruit (undried) bu	55	22,00

Total in foreign vessels	$1,234,249,12
Total in American vessels	753,708,45
Grand Total	$1,987,957,57

Statement of free goods imported into the District of Buffalo Creek during the year 1855, under the tariff of 1846, in American vessels:

Articles.	Value.
Personal Effects	$6,193 00
Timothy seed	359 38
Property of United States returned	19,837 96
Old Junk	224 50
Animals for breed	242 00
Total in American Vessels	$24,856 84

Statement of free goods imported into the District of Buffalo Creek during the year 1855, under the Tariff of 1846, in foreign vessels:

Articles.	Value.
Personal Effects	$7,788,25
Property of United States returned	26,934 63
Timothy seed	469 30
Old Junk	266 00
Copper Ore (164½ tons)	5,766 00
Total in foreign vessels	$41,224 18
Total in American vessels	24,856 84
Grand total	$66,081 02

Statement of dutiable goods imported into the District of Buffalo Creek from the time the Reciprocity Treaty took effect until the 31st December, 1855, in foreign vessels:

Articles.	Quantity.	Value.	Duties.
Scrap Iron lbs	1,608,78		482,63
Old Copper lbs	172	35,26	1,76
Old Brass lbs	50	5,13	26
Molasses gals	10	5,13	1,54
Leather		1,80	36
Shingles no	63½	11.365	34,10
Shingle bolts cords	121	518,14	155,44
Wool lbs	1,382	283,31	84.99
Beeswax lbs	32	5,58	1,12
Wagons no	1	15,38	461
Medicines		14,47	4,54
Scotch Bar Iron cwt	412	975,49	292,65
Axe handles no	12	154	46
Staves no	136,194	2,295,14	459,02
Scow Loat no	1	307,50	92,25
Ale galls	160	33,85	10,15
Castings lbs	526	43,86	13,16
Carts no	2	27,68	8,30
Harness setts	2	41,00	12,30
Total in foreign vessels		$6,332,67	$1661,44
Total in American vessels		2,921,32	724,43
Grand Total		$9,253,99	$2,385,87

Statement of dutiable goods imported into the District of Buffalo Creek from the time the Reciprocity Treaty took effect until the 31st December. 1855, in American vessels:

Articles.	Quantity.	Value.	Duties.
Scrap Iron		552 17	165 65
Old Copper, lbs	565	77 14	3 85
Old Brass	420	53 81	2 69
Last Blocks		32 54	9 76
Shingle Bolts, cords	133	422 56	126 76
Old Type, lbs	100	9 23	1 85
Shingles, (Shaved) No	100,400	354 76	106 43
Hay, lbs	5,000	30 74	6 14
Feathers, lbs	26	13 32	3 33
Hogs, No	1	10 25	3 08
Wagon, No	1	41 00	12 30
Harness Setts	2	17 42	5 22
Furniture		7 69	2 31
Cards, Pkgs	24	3 08	92
Cotton Manufactures, yds	69	11 59	2 89
Cigars, No	3,200	32 80	13 12
Sugar, lbs	50	5 13	1 54
Books, Vols	66	30 26	3 02
Small Boat	1	30 75	9 23
Honey, lbs	40	4 30	1 29
Cider, bbls	3	5 38	1 08
Staves, No	75,562	1,098 16	219 63
Hoops, No	3,900	9 99	3 00
Ale, galls	90	12 30	3 69
Ale, doz. bottles	10	10 25	3 07
Port Wine, galls	5	5 13	2 05
Fig Blue, lbs	100	12 30	2 46
Beds and Bedding	1	5 13	1 54
Confectionary, lbs	240	20 91	6 27
Sundries, bbls	1	1 23	25
Total in American Vessels		$2,921 32	$724 43

Abstract of domestic produce and manufactures exported from the District of Buffalo Creek, N. Y., to Canada, during the year ending December 31st, 1855:

Articles.	Quantity.	Value.
Flour, bbls	2,639	$22,474
Corn Meal, bbls	481	1,633
Pork, bbls	791	12,558
Beef, "	133	2,063
Fish, "	151	1,705
Fish, (dried and smoked) lbs	17,556	1,274
Wheat, bu	25,500	44,622
Corn, bu	100,710	81,173
Oats, Rye and other small grains	55,076	30
Butter, lbs	2,350	
Cheese, lbs	92,829	8
Lard, lbs	21,689	2
Tallow, lbs	162,060	13
Bacon, lbs	121,661	11
Horses, No	51	4
Cattle, No	36	1
Coal, tons	1,004	5
Hides, No	191	
Whiskey, galls	95,116	32
Oil, (whale and other fish) galls	11,729	11
Oil, (lard) galls	505	
Sperm Candles, lbs	1,880	
Boards and scantling, feet	124,579	2
Manufactures of Wood		29
Tar and pitch, bbls	308	1
Biscuit and Ship Bread	109	
Apples, bbls	341	
Potatoes, bu	306	
Onions bu	47	
Skins and Furs, Pkgs		3
Rice, tcs	64	1
Sugar, lbs	54,550	4
Molasses, gals	7,395	4
Vinegar, bbls	90	
Beer, Ale Porter and Cider	82	
Linseed Oil, galls	2,158	2
Spirits of Turpentine, bbls	45	1
Household Furniture		62
Carriages, and parts of		6
Hats, cases	199	6
Boots and Shoes, pairs	19,729	30
Wearing Apparel		3
Saddlery		2
Trunks and Valises		1
Soap, lbs	55,951	2
Snuff	2,682	
Tobacco	83,906	16
Candles	42,345	4
Leather, lbs	54,730	10
Cables and Cordage, lbs	28,666	5
Lead, lbs	31,963	2
Salt, bbls	4,730	7
Iron bar, lbs	13,178	
Iron Nails	48,900	2
Iron Castings		29
Iron, manufactures of		209
Copper and Brass, manufactures of		11
Cotton, manufactures of white		5
Cotton, " colored		10
Bags and other manufactures		3
Drugs and Medicines		10
Earthen and Stone Ware		2
Musical Instruments		8
Brooms, doz	499	1
Oil Cloth, yds	2,031	1
Books and Maps		7
Paper and Stationary		3
Paints and Varnish		2
Brick and Lime		1
Manufactures of Fur		2
Manufactures Marble and Stone		11
Glass Ware		5
Oakum		
Tan Bark, cord	54	
Whalebone, lbs	145	
Hemp, lbs		
Chocolate, lbs	701	
Starch, lbs		
Rosin, bbls	73	
Trees, bundles	9	
Clover Seed, bu	228	1
Oysters		

Total Domestic Produce and Manufactures Exported	$846
Total Foreign Merchandise Exported	88
Total Value of Exports for 1855	$935
Total Value of Exports for 1854	1,152
Decrease in 1855	$217

Statement of goods, wares and merchandise remaining in Public Store in

THE CITY OF BUFFALO.

District of Buffalo Creek on the 31st December, 1855:

Articles.	Quantity.	Value.	Duties.
Brandy	2 hlf pipes, 12 qr, 2 eights.	1,043 00	1,043 00
Wine	50 baskets	294 00	113 80
Iron	673½ tons	13,972 78	4,191 84
Crockery	10 hhds, 351 crates	11,958 95	3,587 68
Total		$27,268 73	$8,936 32

Abstract of foreign merchandise exported from the District of Buffalo Creek, N. Y. to Canada during the year ending December 1st, 1855:

Articles.	Quantity.	Value.
Coffee lbs	65,665	6,640
Tea lbs	89,446	66,525
Raisins lbs	6,264	676
Pepper lbs	5,691	709
Tin Plate boxes	129	1,324
Prunes lbs	2,150	237
Currants lbs	2,216	226
Figs lbs	3,250	374
Nuts lbs	11,511	1157
Rice lbs	6,026	635
Ginger lbs	3,392	342
Crockery pkgs	.....	2,647
Fruit boxes	151	763
Refined sugar lbs	50,693	6,067
Clover lbs	700	170
Total Foreign Merchandise exported in 1855		$88,492
Total Foreign Merchandise exported in 1854		105,301
Showing a decrease last year of		$16,809

The annual duties collected at Buffalo for series of years, are as follows:

1846	$12,389 78	1851	$92,357 69
1847	24,361 78	1852	69,723 74
1848	21,236 30	1853	84,943 33
1849	46,939 86	1854	99,663 59
1850	67,649 95	1855	29,275 40

Statement showing the value of domestic and foreign produce and merchandise exported in American and foreign vessels during the year 1855:

Domestic produce and merchandise in American vessels	$447,093
Do. do do in Foreign vessels	393,591
Excess in American vessels	47,502
Foreign merchandise in American vessels	53,141
" " " Foreign "	35,351
Excess in American vessels	17,790

Statement of goods and merchandise withdrawn from warehouse in the District of Buffalo Creek for warehousing in other districts, for exportation and for consumption during the year 1855:

Articles.	Quantity.	Dutiable Value.	Duties.
Flour bbls	165	1,183 87	236,72
Wheat bu	6,665	9,560 76	1,912 95
Crockery (crates)	706	28,803 05	8,668 82
Lumber ft	135,108	984 12	178 82
Codfish quintals	50	152 00	30 40
Brandy casks	28	269 70	2,696 70
Sugar hhds	21	1,589 66	278 90
Pig Iron tons	753	10,008 77	3,002 63
Gloves & Jackets	1	170 00	51 00
Hardware cases	10	1,375 00	412 00
Total		$54,096 93	$17,468 94

Statement of goods and merchandise transferred from other Districts to the District of Buffalo Creek, in bond for warehousing and export to Canada during the year 1855:

Articles.	Quantity.	Value.
Sugar hhds	1,092	$45,488
Raisins boxes	655	875
Linseed Oil casks	12	937
Calf Skins boxes	2	384
Wine pkgs	147	966
Porter casks	50	484
Brandy casks	3	277
Dry Goods	.....	16,106
Cigars	.....	953
Hardware	.....	1,488
Blank Note Forms	.....	1,514
Blank Books	.....	892
Hides	.....	413
Sundries	.....	664
Total value		$71,441

The Erie Canal.

The returns of the trade of the Erie Canal at this point show a steady increase from year to year in the quantity and value of most articles sent to and received from tide water. In some articles, such as flour, beef, wool, lumber, etc., which our tables of receipts by Lake and State Line Rail Road, show a handsome increase, the amount transported by the Canal, exhibits a considerable decrease. For instance, the receipts of flour from the west by Lake and Rail Road and the shipments by Canal for the past two years, exhibits the following result:

	Receipts.	Canal Exports.
1854	750,535	288,124
1855	1,003,906	235,578

Here it will be seen that while there is an increase in the receipts last year, as compared with 1854, of 253,371 bbls.; there is a decrease of 52,546 bbls. in the shipments by Canal. Again, in the article of beef, the total receipts show an increase last year, as compared with 1854, of 43,794 bbls.; while the shipments by Canal show an increase of only 8,175 bbls. This comparison will hold good on a large number of articles which legitimately belong to the Canal, but which have been diverted to the railroads.

The time has now arrived in the history of our Canals, when their revenue fails to meet the requirements of the Constitution. There is now a large deficit which will probably have to be made up by a direct tax. This is to be attributed to the railroads, and to them only. The facts show this conclusively, and there is no evading them. The following will show the probable amount of produce shipped east by the New York Central and New York City Rail Roads during the year:

660,628 bbls. flour, the toll on which is	$155,823
65,000 " beef, " " " "	24,133
40,000 " pork, " " " "	7,424
200,000 bu. wheat, " " " "	13,104
2,500,000 lbs. butter and cheese	2,184
15,000,000 " bacon, lard and ta low,	8,190
5,000,000 " wool	7,280
On other articles not enumerated,	30,000
Total on down freight	$948,138
The up freight on both roads amounts to about 100,000 tons; the toll, at 4 mills, is	291,200
Total tolls lost to the State,	$539,338

On cattle, horses, sheep, hogs, hides, leather, &c. we have made no computation or even estimate of the toll they would have had to pay had they been shipped by Canal. We estimate that the down and up tonnage of the several other railroads in the State, and the tolls thereon about equal to that on the New York Central and New York City roads, and we have a grand total loss of tolls to the State of over $1,000,000. This is the premium paid by the State to these railroads, that they may successfully prevent the enlargement of the Erie and other Canals.

We have shown by the above that these roads are yearly diverting enough of the legitimate business of the Canals, if tolls were collected thereon, to more than pay the interest on the entire cost of the enlargement of the Canals, as contemplated by the Constitution. A diversity of opinion exists as to I ow the deficiency should be made up. It is contended first, that railroads should be tolled; second, that a system of discriminating tolls should be adopted making produce passing the Welland Canal pay the same toll from Oswego as it would from Buffalo; third, that it should be met by a direct tax; and fourth, that the tolls should be reduced so low as to bring back the trade diverted to the railroads. These several propositions all have their advocates. The reduction of tolls tends to cheapen transportation, and the lower the freight tariffs are put, a greater extent of country is enabled to send their surplus products to market.

With a two mill toll on flour, butter, wheat, wool, etc., if facts are of any value, the greater portion of those article that went forward on the railroads from this point last year, would have gone by canal. The State would have lost on most of those articles one-third of the tolls paid and have gained two-thirds on those carried by railroads. We fear that unless the tolls are reduced on the Canal, or tolls are imposed on railroads, or a system of discrimination adopted, the predictions of the enemies of the Canals in times past will soon be more than realized.

Statement of Property first cleared at the Collector's Office at Buffalo on the Erie Canal, during the year 1855, showing the quantity and average value of each article and also the whole amount of tolls received at that office on boats and each article of property, during the same period.

Articles.	Quantity.	Value of each article.	Tolls on each article
BOATS.			
Toll at 2 cents			$41,378
THE FOREST.			
Product of Wood.			
Boards & Sc'tl'g ft	48,989,289	979,786	76,955
Shingles, M	766	3,064	83
Timber, 100 c ft	216	32	3
Staves, lbs	149,212,261	596,849	43,451
Ashes pot and pearl	4,808	125,008	3,200
Total value		1,704,739	123,694
AGRICULTURE.			
Product of Animals.			
Pork, bbls	72,278	1,301,004	11,593
Beef	34,925	488,950	10,520
Bacon, lbs	6,794,919	645,517	3,793
Cheese	601,223	60,122	265
Butter	241,352	48,403	223
Lard, Tallow and Lard Oil	5,169,128	620,295	4,837
Wool	2,766,498	995,939	2,918
Hides	853,694	51,222	737
Total value		$4,206,492	34,889
Vegetable Food.			
Flour, bbls	235,578	2,002,413	39,372
Wheat, bush	6,455,641	11,620,154	215,051
Rye	221,497	254,722	11,917
Corn	7,713,451	6,410,732	224,701
Corn meal, bbls	1,251	4,344	114
Barley, bush	24,390	31,707	1,000
Oats	2,287,950	1,143,975	37,668
Bran and ship stuffs, lbs	4,749,587	28,498	1,810
Peas and beans bu	689	1,206	55
Potatoes	812	406	
Dried Fruit, lbs	16,741	1,841	3
Total value		$21,529,998	$531,697
All other Agricultural Products.			
Cotton, lbs	15,715	1,572	1
Unmanufactured tobacco	1,869,402	149,552	407
Hemp	136,455	10,916	8
Clover & grass seed	710,469	63,942	827
Flax seed	420,319	14,711	317
Hops	10,811	2,162	
Total value		$242,855	1,462
		$25,979,345	568,049

THE CITY OF BUFFALO.

MANUFACTURES.

Domestic spirits, gals	759,333	280,964	4,700 65
Oil meal & cake, lbs.	4,383,403	65,751	2,403 23
Leather	459,554	110,293	158 63
Furniture	226,982	27,238	245 72
Bar and pig lead	2,340,437	152,128	298 57
Pig iron	475,471	9,509	2 94
Bloom & bar iron	338,970	11,864	117 83
Castings & iron ware	105,585	4,223	24 67
Domestic salt	752,650	2,916	2 48
Total value		$665,886	7,954 73

MERCHANDISE,

Iron and Steel, lbs	759,575	60,766	117 90
Railroad Iron	1,055,001	34,815	509 03
Flint enamel crockery & glass ware	67,406	6,741	50 28
All other merchandise	1,030,704	72,149	1,163 01
Total value		$174,471	1,840 22

OTHER ARTICLES.

Stone, lime and clay	5,668,655	11,337	1,498 96
Mineral coal	21,776,110	76,216	1,910 23
Copper Ore	310,736	108,758	33 19
Sundries	10,753,698	537,685	9,215 18
Total value		$733,996	12,657 56
Grand total value		$29,258,437	$755,574 50

MANUFACTURES.

Furniture	6,523,586	782,830
Pig Iron	22,808,980	457,189
Castings and Iron Ware	33,350,562	1,333,022
Domestic Cottons	1,447,669	521,101
Domestic Salt	109,084,542	654,567
Foreign Salt	240,769	1,826
Total Value		$4,205,180

MERCHANDIZE.

Sugar, lbs	49,368,103	5,689,970
Molasses	16,113,013	773,425
Coffee	13,982,797	2,097,420
Nails, Spikes and Horse Shoes	6,378,723	318,936
Iron and Steel	24,413,763	2,185,093
Railroad Iron	59,567,908	1,769,877
Flint Enamel, Crockery and Glass Ware	9,009,338	991,027
All other Merchandize	109,618,022	67,847,209
Total Value		$80,672,957

OTHER ARTICLES.

Live Cattle, Hogs and Sheep	7,130	357
Stone, Lime and Clay	46,290,406	92,581
Gypsum	862,032	8,620
Mineral Coal	86,080,874	301,283
Sundries	22,742,838	1,591,999
Value		$1,994,840
Grand Total Value		$87,856,037

Statement of property left at Buffalo on the Erie Canal, or which was left between that place and the Collector's Office next in order on the Canal; showing the quantity and average value of each article during the year 1855:

Articles.	Quantity.	Value of each article.
THE FOREST.		
Product of Wood.		
Boards and Scantling, feet	8,424,871	168,497
Shingles, M	251	1,004
Timber, 100 c feet	297,079	44,562
Wood, cord	24,660	96,310
Ashes, pot and pearl, bbls	10	260
Total Value		$300,633
AGRICULTURE.		
Product of Animals.		
Pork, bbls	9	162
Wool	6,689	2,408
Hides	724,055	72,405
Value		$74,975
Vegetable Food.		
Flour, bbls	36,051	306,434
Wheat, bush	44,283	79,769
Corn	3,250	2,714
Barley	81,584	106,059
Bran and ship stuffs, lbs	600,064	3,600
Peas and Beans, bush	32	126
Potatoes	12,192	6,096
Dried Fruit, lbs	564,235	62,066
Value		$566,804
All other Agricultural Products.		
Hemp, lbs	14,528	1,170
Clover and Grass Seed	12,250	1,103
Hops	191,877	38,375
Value		$40,648
Total Value		$682,427
MANUFACTURES.		
Domestic Spirits, galls	1,520	562
Oil meal and cake, lbs	18,166	272
Leather	1,886,336	452,720

Below we give a comparative table showing the quantities of some of the leading articles which have been first cleared from this place during the past three years:

Articles.	1853.	1854.	1855.
Flour, bbls	658,354	288,124	235,578
Pork	86,085	123,255	72,278
Beef	49,346	26,750	34,925
Wheat, bu	4,958,818	2,811,687	6,455,641
Corn	3,118,691	9,405,859	7,713,451
Oats	1,163,599	4,134,298	2,287,950
Barley	257,238	206,477	24,390
Rye	59,727	127,929	221,497
Tobacco	3,391,133	6,323,050	1,869,402
Whiskey, galls	1,837,711	990,270	759,563
Hemp, lbs	676,317	1,910,399	136,455
Butter, lbs	739,192	341,609	241,352
Cheese	2,055,737	597,792	601,223
Wool	4,262,356	2,369,573	2,766,498
Boards and scantling	61,885,663	59,109,520	48,989,289
Staves, lbs	76,066,058	120,343,262	149,212,261
Sundries	9,056,076	9,057,081	10,953,698

The annexed table will show some of the leading articles ascending the canal, and landed at Buffalo during the past three years:

Articles.	1853.	1854.	1855
Merchandise	132,303,044	147,381,724	169,618,022
Sugar	28,912,488	18,875,883	49,368,103
Molasses	14,305,967	10,075,455	16,113,013
Coffee	4,772,489	14,042,671	13,982,297
Nails, spikes & horse shoes	9,824,477	9,381,987	6,378,723
Iron and steel	11,794,300	22,913,262	27,413,763
Railway iron	123,743,264	147,322,490	59,567,908
Crockery & glassware	11,672,849	10,921,591	9,009,333
Sundries	2,502,559	22,729,898	22,742,888
Flour, bbls	43,751	9,660	36,051
Wheat, bu		18,540	44,283
Barley bu	2,773	18,862	81,584
Boards & scantling	3,658,715	2,723,096	8,424,871
Timber feet	1,151,356	145,098	297,079
Wood, cords	34,517	25,692	24,660
Wool, lbs	34,047	4,700	6,589
Hides, lbs	1,092,120	983,315	724,055
Hops bls	128,429	215,734	191,877
Leather	1,549,044	1,968,806	1,886,336

Pig Iron	13,763,460	14,449,254	22,858,980
Castings and Iron Ware	27,687,945	25,879,507	33,350,562
Domestic Cottons	1,031,459	2,886,031	1,447,669
Domestic salt	59,205,314	66,487,871	109,084,542
Foreign salt	122,160	1,049,291	240,769
Mineral coal	46,626,510	70,627,649	86,080,874

In down freights there has been a falling off in flour, pork, corn, oats, barley, tobacco, whiskey, hemp, butter, boards and scantling, &c., while there is an increase in beef, wheat, rye, wool, staves and sundries — This decrease as we have already remarked, is to be attributable to the large amount of those articles which have been sent forward by railroad.

The value of the exports by canal as made up at the Canal Collector's Office for 1855 is

	$29,258,437
Total value for 1854	26,936,707
An increase in favor of 1855 of	$2,321,730
The am't of tolls collected the past year was	$755,574 50
The amount collected in 1854	685,315 35
Showing an increase this year of	$70,259 15
And an increase over 1853 of	60,209 79

In the articles of up freight it will be observed that there is a large increase in merchandise, sugar, molasses, iron and steel, barley, boards, timber, pig iron, castings and iron ware, domestic salt and mineral coal, and a decline in coffee, railroad iron, crockery and glass ware.

The value of the imports as made up at the Collectors Office for

1855 was	$87,856,037
And for the year 1854	77,035,271
Showing an increase of	$10,820,766

The whole amount of tonnage delivered in Buffalo in

1849 was	211,047	tons.
1850 was	260,923	"
1851 was	237,351	"
1852 was	337,620	"
1853 was	438,786	"
1854 was	380,772	"
1855 was	404,108	"

The following is a comparative statement of the duration of navigation on the Erie Canal for a period of ten years:

Year.	Opened.	Closed.	Days Open.
1844	April 18	November 26	223
1845	April 15	November 29	228
1846	April 16	November 25	224
1847	May 1	December 1	214
1848	May 1	December 9	223
1849	May 1	December 5	219
1850	April 22	December 5	228
1851	April 15	December 5	235
1852	April 20	December 15	239
1853	April 20	December 15	239
1854	May 1	December 3	217
1855	May 1	December 5	219

Early in the spring of 1855 the "American Transportation Company" was organized to navigate the canal and Lakes with a capital of $900,000. This company was composed of nine forwarding firms, and they own twenty-two propellers and some five hundred canal boats. By this organization they were enabled to transport a large amount of tonnage, at a much less expense than under the old system, and were better able to compete with the railroads in the carrying trade. This winter another and similar company has been formed with a like capital, under the name of the "Western Transportation Company," and they control twenty propellers, six sail vessels and about two hundred canal boats.

These two companies, organized as they are, and being managed by men who have been all their lives connected with the trade of the Lakes and Canal, and having their agents in every port on the Lakes must exert a powerful influence in controlling the carrying trade of the Lakes and bringing it to this point to be re-shipped by their lines on the canals to the seaboard.— The canal during the past season has been in unusually good order, and the detentions from breaks or low water were but of seldom occurrence. In canal boat building the amount of business done last year was quite limited. Under the new organization less new boats were required to transact the business of the canals, and a large number of the larger class were added the year before. Van Slyke, Notter & Co. have built twelve new boats during the year, at a cost of about $20,600. Mr. McMillen built two boats and one scow at a cost of about $4,000. Mr. S. C. Jones built one, and Mr. Howell has lengthened several boats. At present there is but little doing in any of the yards in this branch of trade, although contracts are about concluded for building several boats to be ready early in the spring.

Below we present a statement of the canal business of Black Rock, which is within our city limits, and which should be included in the business of Buffalo. Most of the produce reported as first cleared from Black Rock, was shipped at this port and re-cleared at that office.

Statement of property first cleared from ~~th~~e Collector's Office at Black Rock, on the ~~E~~rie Canal, during the year 1855, showing ~~th~~e quantity and value of each article:

Articles.	Quantity.	Value.
~~Fl~~our, bbls	99,017	$841,644
~~C~~orn Meal, bbls	41	144
~~Po~~rk, bbls	472	8,496
~~Be~~ef, bbls	1	14
~~As~~hes, bbls	47	306
~~W~~heat, bu	43,982	79,168
~~R~~ye, bu	100	115
~~Co~~rn, bu	36,740	30,678
~~Ba~~rley, bu	4,215	5,479
~~O~~ats, bu	6,549	3,275
~~Pe~~as, bu	4	7
~~Po~~tatoes, bu	325	162
~~B~~ran and Shipstuffs, lbs	2,052,096	12,313
~~Ba~~con, lbs	153,600	14,592
~~B~~utter, lbs	447	80
~~La~~rd, Tallow and Lard Oil	41,275	4,953
~~W~~ool	11,257	4,053
~~Bo~~ards and Scantling, feet	5,467,786	109,356
~~Sh~~ingles, M	2	8
~~T~~imber, c feet	123,182	18,477
~~S~~taves, bundles	932,510	3,730
~~F~~ire Wood, cords	10,412	36,442
~~To~~bacco, lbs	10,620	850
~~Se~~eds, lbs	11,876	950
~~D~~omestic Spirits, galls	13,630	5,043
~~L~~ead, (pig) lbs	67,130	3,021
~~B~~loom and Bar Iron, lbs	1,465,000	51,275
~~Ca~~stings and Iron Ware, lbs	54,000	2,160
~~N~~ails, Spikes and Horse Shoes, lbs	1,068,000	57,672
~~St~~one, Lime and Clay	15,368,140	30,736
~~M~~ineral Coal	140,000	420
~~Su~~ndries	710,584	55,529
Total Value		$1,361,999
Total Tons		66,902
Total Tolls		$97,679 10

Statement of property left at Black ~~R~~ock, on the Erie Canal, showing the quantity and value during the year 1855:

Articles.	Quantity.	Value.
~~F~~lour, bbls	380	$3,230
~~C~~orn Meal, bbls	6	21
~~Po~~rk, bbls	9	162
~~W~~heat, bu	478,598	861,476
~~R~~ye	6,170	7,096
~~C~~orn	21,025	17,536
~~O~~ats	2,433	1,216
~~Pe~~as and Beans	12	21
~~Po~~tatoes	310	155
~~La~~rd, Tallow and Lard Oil, lbs	11,172	1,341
~~B~~oards and Scantling, feet	1,234,922	24,968
~~S~~hingles, M	452	208
~~T~~imber, c feet	128,344	19,252
~~S~~taves, bdls	152,000	608
~~W~~ood, cords	2,120	7,420
~~F~~urs and Peltry, lbs	12,000	1,800
~~D~~omestic Spirits galls	393	145
~~Ir~~on (pig) lbs	3,705,432	55,581
~~B~~loom and Bar Iron, lbs	484,605	19,961
~~C~~astings and Iron Ware, lbs	2,502,990	100,119
~~D~~omestic Salt, lbs	584,475	3,507
~~S~~ugar, lbs	22,117	2,101
~~M~~olasses	12,504	600
~~C~~offee, lbs	1,247	162
~~N~~ails, Spikes and Horse Shoes	5,880	318
~~Ir~~on and Steel, lbs	971,772	77,742
~~A~~ll other Merchandise	98,852	6,920
~~S~~tone, Lime and Clay	21,554,029	43,108
~~G~~ypsum	3,200	80
~~M~~ineral Coal	5,832,300	17,497
~~Su~~ndries	2,451,243	122,562
Total Value		$1,395,846
Total Tons		45,453

Railroads.

In compiling our annual statement of the year's business, on the several lines of Railroad terminating at this point, we are unable to present anything satisfactory with the exception of the Buffalo and Erie or State Line Railroad, the officers of which road have afforded us every facility we could wish, and we would here return our thanks to the Gen. Freight Agent Mr. Starin, and his deputy Mr. Stark, for many favors shown us.

Under the old law the Railroads in our State were obliged to report the total amount of produce, merchandise, &c., carried by them over their road, while under the present law they are only obliged to make their returns for the year ending 30th September, showing the total quantities of products of forest, animals, vegetable food, agricultural productions, manufactures, merchandise and miscellaneous articles carried to and from all stations for the year. Under this classification it is impossible to tell how much flour, grain, live stock, provisions, or merchandise has been transported from any one point. For the past five years excepting last year, we have been permitted to use the freight books of all the roads terminating here, and from these we have after several days hard labor, been able to make up tables showing the exact amount of freight of every description carried over the road. The enormous increase from year to year in the quantity transported over the lines extending to New York, freight that legitimately belonged to the canal, but which was diverted from that channel by ruinous rates on the railroads and on which the State was constantly loosing large sums in the shape of tolls began to awaken the attention of the people of the State to the importance of either tolling the railroads or reducing the tolls on the canal, so as to bring back that trade. The managers of the railroads in view of these facts, have withheld their books from us and we are therefore unable to give the exact amount of the freight transported by them, but are able to approximate very near to it by taking our total receipts by Lake and State Line Railroad from the West and deducting the amount carried by canal and estimating that consumed in the city. This we have done in the articles of flour and grain, and we will here add that all the live stock brought to this city as well as nearly all the beef, lard butter, cheese, tallow, wool, whiskey, hides, &c., is sent east by railroad. The present Railroad law should be amended, and the several roads compelled to make a full and correct report of the freight transported by them both through and way, precisely similar to the annual statements made up of the trade of the canals. There is no good reason why it should not be done. It would be but a trifling expense to the roads and would prove more satisfactory to the public.

Buffalo and Erie Railroad.

This road which has scarcely been in operation four years, is probably the best paying road in the country. It is managed in every department by gentlemen experienced in railroad matters, and its annual traffic has increased from year to year beyond all precedent. We have in our former statements referred to the facilities this road possesses in the shape of equipments, depots, &c., for the transaction of its enormous business, and all that it now needs to enable it to work to advantage and accommodate its growing traffic is a double track between this city and Cleveland. By an arrangement entered into with the several railroads in Ohio, Indiana and other western States the cars of these several roads are loaded at stations on those roads with produce for this city and the same cars are here reloaded with merchandise for those same stations and for other roads connecting with them but of a different guage. This we believe is not generally understood. It saves not only time and labor in loading and unloading at the end of each road, but insures greater expedition in transporting produce or merchandise to its destination. To show the advantage of this system it is only necessary to state that during the past year cars of other roads in the west have travelled 1,575,238 miles on this road which is of itself only 100 miles in length.

The following will show the freight earnings of the Buffalo & State Line Railroad for each month and year, from the opening of the road in 1852 to December 31, 1855.

	1852.	1853.	1854.	1855.
January		16,105 42	18,078 04	44,009
February		15,706 14	26,002 02	35,582
March	5,795 80	21,572 23	44,393 30	53,278
April	9,576 35	11,541 06	30,252 08	47,211
May	5,861 49	5,623 45	12,706 74	20,065
June	2,271 00	5,176 08	13,585 03	17,735
July	2,401 85	4,728 23	10,888 62	15,929
August	1,971 22	3,736 17	12,733 58	17,597
September	2,562 27	4,316 45	12,850 49	18,754
October	5,07 436	7,350 32	18,120 09	24,026
November	4,837 41	9,500 05	22,316 92	43,731
December	10,089 47	9,589 33	47,547 45	64,411
	$50,441 22	114,944 93	269,474 36	402,330

The amount of freight in pounds transported from all stations each way over the road for the years 1854 and 1855, was as follows:

```
1855----------------------------------358,903,125
1854----------------------------------147,769,955
       Increase in 1855---------------211,133,170
```

The increase is about 150 per cent. Of the above amount for 1855 the through and way freight bears the following proportion:

```
Through freight lbs----------------305,528,668
Way freight lbs--------------------- 53,374,457
   Total---------------------------358,903,125
```

The number of pounds carried one mile was----------------------------21,944,580,360

The total passenger and freight earnings during the year ending 30th Sept., 1853 were $679,750, and for the year ending on same day in 1854, $507,618 showing an increase in favor of 1855 of $172,132 over 1854.

The following will show the amount of freight transported over the Buffalo & Erie Railroad to and from all stations for the year 1855.

```
Products of the Forest lbs-----------  15,007,849
Products of animals lbs-------------- 191,949,275
Vegetable food lbs-------------------  27,422,072
All other agricultural products------   2,895,671
Manufactures ------------------------  18,858,344
Merchandise -------------------------  96,287,814
Miscellaneous -----------------------   6,482,100
   Total---------------------------- 358,903,125
```

Below we give a statement of the amount of produce brought to this city during the year by this road. It shows an enormous increase in the quantity of flour, pork, seeds, cattle, hogs, wool, &c., an increase in value of over $4,570,000 as compared with 1854 and an increase over 1853 of $8,734,111.

Statement showing the principal articles of produce brought to this city by the Buffalo and Erie Railroad during the years 1853, 1854 and 1855, with the value of that transported for 1855:

THE CITY OF BUFFALO. 39

	1853.	1854.	1855.	Value in 1855.
ur, bbls	156	10,724	66,683	$566,805
rk	198	2,081	10,715	187,512
ef	89	552	2,593	35,005
niskey	171	4,785	8,697	119,152
eds	5,828	15,577	10,475	104,750
hes	103	69	107	2,782
gs	1,370	2,488	2,029	24,328
ttle, bbls	13,482	43.210	51,170	4,093,600
rses	423	353	375	37,500
eep	4,482	11,600	36,670	110,010
gs, live	26,640	83,280	194,240	2,330,880
gs, dressed	7,003	6,031	12,179	182,685
tter, lbs	1,151,700	769,700	679,400	135,880
eese	71,900	441,844	552,900	55,290
con	77,000	320,120	1,144,120	137,294
rd	99,400	411,200	2,138,300	213,830
llow	46,800	642,600	820,400	73,836
ease		157,300	184,400	14,752
ool, bales	1,294	4,498	6,818	409,080
lts	1,848	2,351	13,502	270,040
mp	262	60	558	13,950
ax	50	198	180	5,400
ins		789	1,110	55,500
ather, rolls	1,785	2,772	3,987	99,675
des, No	964	3,777	33,557	134,228
n, tons	200	47	171	6,840
bacco, hhds	21	83	94	5,640
bacco, boxes	97	106	258	6,450
mber, feet		5,630,000	4,050,000	101,200
ves, No		125,000	120,000	3,600
ingles, bun's		3,724	5,551	16,653
th, M		104,000	200,000	400
l, bbls		688	2,718	122,270
ied Fruit		2,381	1,545	15,450
ples		3,093	2,395	2,395
sh		15	450	3,150
ans		297	600	1,200
gar, hhds		23	205	15,375
oom Corn, bls		241	1,613	19,356
rs		60	105	15,750
gs, sacks		2,329	2,111	21,110
ndles, boxes		1,609	2,565	12,825
assware		854	888	5,328
per, bundles		7,983	10,564	62,820
tatoes, bush		31,351	1,573	786
athers, bags		278	532	6,384
ed, bush		3,016	801	400
tton, bales			129	6,450
al, tons			1,970	9,850
ap, boxes			50	300
heat, bush			24,265	43,677
rley, bush			15,341	17,652
e, bush			19,864	21,850
ts. bush			8,832	3,532
lasses, bbls			152	1,520
ts, bbls			855	4,275
arch, boxes			2,540	6,350
arch, bbls			132	3,300
ir, Pkgs			108	432
ndries, Pkgs				1,000,000

Total Value for 1855 .... $10,968,384
" " " 1854 6,397,923
" " " 1853 2,234,273

Increase in 1855 over 1854 .... $4,570,461

New York Central Rail Road.

It has been our custom, in former years, to present in our Annual Statement, a table showing the amount of produce shipped from this point east by the New York Central Rail Road. This table we have always made up from the down freight books of the road, which we were permitted to use. Last year these books were withheld after the 30th of September, and this year we are not allowed to use them at all. The managers of the road being averse to having the amount of freight transported by their road made public.— We have, however given under the head of "Erie Canal," and in the review of the produce trade, an estimate of the amount of flour, grain and provisions carried by this road during the year.

The total number of tons of freight transported by this road during
1855 was .... 670,073 tons.
1854 " .... 549,805 "

Increase in 1855, ... 120,268

This increase is principally in flour, beef, pork, wool and wheat, carried east, and merchandise brought from New York.

As we have in former statements referred to the facilities which this road possesses for doing an immense freighting business, with its depots, docks, elevators, etc., we will content ourselves this year by simply giving the following facts, condensed from the annual report of the Company for the year ending September 30th, last:

Earnings and Receipts:
From passengers $3,242,229 19
From freight 3,189,602 90
From other sources 131,749 05

Total $6,563,581 14

Payments other than for Construction:
For transportation expenses, viz:
For passenger business $1,861,544 12
For freight business 1,539,911 53
                                              $3,401,455 65
For interest on funded debt ... $339,928 10
For account debt certificate sinking fund 111,182 38
                                              $951,110 43

Total $4,352,566 13
For Dividends, Nos. 3 and 4 .... $1,919,484 00
For Dividend No. 2, deferred from last year .. 956,283 08

Of the expenses $78,360 79 were for repairs of machinery, $836,562 56 for maintaining roadway and $1,786,532 30 for operating the road. To bring the report up to the 1st of December, 1855, the Directors made a comparative statement of the earnings of the Road for October and November:

OCTOBER.	1854.	1855.
Passengers	$395,022 15	$354,815 80
Freight	254,397 97	372,542 63
Mails, &c		8,953 14
Total	$649,420 12	$736,311 57
Increase		$36,891 45

NOVEMBER.	1854.	1855.
Passengers	$281,025 19	$274,966 59
Freight	236,201 32	394,160 75
Mails, &c		3,754 01
Total	567,227 01	676,881 35
Increase		109,654 34

In both these months the increase was entirely in freight earnings. The passenger earnings show a falling off of $46,264 95. Of the aggregate increase in the year ending Sept. 30, 1855, over 1854— 645,246,64—only $90,915 30 was from passengers.

The total number of passengers transported during the year ending 30th Sept., was 2,717, 477, of which 2,515,943 were way, and 201,534 were through. The number of tons of freight transported was 670,073. The Company own 188 locomotives and 2,425 cars of all descriptions.

The total capital stock is	24,154,360 69
Last report	23,067,415 00
Increase in 1855	1,087,445 69
Funded debt	14,462,742 32
Last report	11,947,121 04
Increase in 1855	2,515,621 23
Increase of stock and debt in 1855	3,603,066 97

The amount of freight carried from this point eastward during the year is estimated to value about $15,000,000. The amount of up freight received here is estimated at about 100,000 tons, principally dry goods, groceries and general merchandise and is valued at $35,000,000.

Buffalo and New York City Rail Road.

The Buffalo and New York City Rail Road passed into the hands of the New York and Erie Rail Road Company on the 1st of September last, under a lease for a term of years. The terms of the lease are very easy, the Buffalo and N. Y. City Road receiving no rent unless the operating of their road pays a profit. A separate account is to be kept with that portion of the route which is charged with all expenses, use of equipage, repairs, etc. The Erie Company will have nothing to pay unless there is a surplus over all this. By this arrangement one of the principal obstacles to a good understanding with the Central was removed, as the Erie now have full control of the entire line between Jerser City and Buffalo. It is a very judicious arrangement both for the Erie and Hornellsville road.

Passengers and freight now pass directly through from Buffalo to New York, without change of cars or transhipment at Hornellsville. The effect will be to make Buffalo instead of Dunkirk, the terminus the New York and Erie Rail Road, as running directly here will involve no additional cost to the company.

The western terminus of the New York and Erie road has been at the wrong place Buffalo, from its position, and the wealth invested here in the forwarding trade must be the great depot for the transhipment of freight from the west, and it is useless to attempt to divert the business that legitimately belongs to it, to a port like Dunkirk. Dunkirk must become to Buffalo what Piermont was to New York, and the Erie road will never succeed in diverting freight and passengers from the Central, to any considerable extent, till it makes this city its western depot.

The route via. the Buffalo and New York City Rail Road to Elmira and Williamsport, thence to Philadelphia and Baltimore needs but to be made generally known throughout the South to attract to it a very large proportion of pleasure travel during the summer; at the same time it will open to the business of the three cities a trade whose magnitude and value can at present scarcely be estimated.

The earnings and expenses of this road for the two past years, ending September 30th, were as follows:

	Earnings.	Expenses.
1855	$288,392	257,496
1854	254,770	192,740
Increase	$33,622	64,756

The net earnings for the year ending September 30th, last, were $30,896; since which time it has been operated by the New York and Erie Rail Road. Since the transfer to the Erie we learn that the business for the remainder of the year shows a handsome increase.

The following will show the business of the road for the years ending July 1st 1854–5:

Earnings from July 1, '53 to July 1, '54	$250,768 9
" " " 1, '54 " 1, '55	291,710 2
Increase of earnings (16 per cent.)	40,941 3
Expense from July 1, '53 to July 1, '54	296,796 1
" " " 1, '54 to " 1, '55	234,739 8
Decrease of expenses (21 per cent.)	62,056 2

The track and rolling stock are worth 15 per cent. more than they were July 1, '54.

Increase of earnings in last year	40,941 3
Decrease of expenses "	62,056 2
In favor of last year	102,997 5

THE CITY OF BUFFAO.   41

...nings from July 1, '53 to July 1, '54, ... 250,768 96
...enses   "   "   "   " 296,796 16

...xpenses more than earnings, ... 46,027 20
...ings from July 1, '54 to July 1, '55, ... 291,710 27
...enses   "   "   "   " 234,739 88

...rnings more than expenses, ... $56,970 39

The value of the freight carried east over ...s road is estimated at $4,000,000; the ...ue of that brought from the east to be ...ut $8,000,000.

Buffalo and Niagara Falls Rail Road.

This road, heretofore under perpetual ...se to the N. Y. Central Company, has ...n consolidated with the latter, and cap...l shares issued to represent the property, ...der a late act of the Legislature. The ...ount is something like $900,000, thus ...reasing the capital of the Central from ...3,085,600 to over twenty-four millions. ...e addition made to the construction ac...nt of the Central for the six months ...ling 31st July, out of means previously ...vided, was less than $190,000, so that ... rumor current in the early part of the ...nmer that the Company would require ...ew loan of one or two millions to com...te their estimates for new work, was ...olly groundless.

This road, which is a branch of the New ...rk Central, is used by the Great West-...n Railway, to the Suspension Bridge, ...ffalo, Brantford and Goderich to Black ...ck, and by the Buffalo, Lockport and ...chester Rail Road Company to Tona...nda. This road does a large freight as ...ll as passenger business.

Buffalo and Corning Rail Road.

This road is in working order from Bata...to Corning. Between Batavia and this ...y the track is graded, but the Company ... being able from want of means to ...cure the iron for this part of the road, ...e left it in an unfinished state. Active ...ertion are now being made, and it is con...ently expected that the entire length of ... road will be in operation during the ...sent year.

The earnings of that portion of the road ...operation were for the year ending Sept. ...h, 1855, $214,524, and the expense ...25,399.

ffalo, Brantford & Goderich Rail Road.

This road has labored under pecuniary ...barrassments during the past year, and has been closed nearly half the time. For want of means the construction of the road from Paris to Goderich has been abandoned for the present, and that part of the road which is completed, namely, from Fort Erie to Paris, has only been in operation for a few weeks, at intervals, during the year. Important changes will most probably be made in the management of this road soon—changes of a character which, if perfected, would place the road in a solvent position, and result in its entire completion to Goderich next year. It seems that the English bond-holders, becoming somewhat alarmed at the reports which had reached them, of the financial condition of the road, sent out a Mr. Robson, an engineer of character, to examine into its affairs and its prospects. From this examination we understand that Mr. R. has come to a most favorable conclusion in reference to the future prosperity of the road, relieved from its present financial difficulties, and completed as designed. The road is capable from its locality, of transacting a large and profitable business; but before it can answer the expectation of its friends, it must be relieved of its present difficulties, and placed in an independent, working condition.

A proposition has been made by an English firm, who represent the holders of the first mortgage bonds, on which no interest has been paid, to take the road for a term of years, finish it to Goderich, pay the interest now due, guarantee it for the future, and place the road in good condition. A large majority of the Directors favor the lease to the new Company, and meetings have been held in the several counties through which the road runs, and all have approved of the contemplated lease. The following facts in reference to the road may be of interest:

ITS PRESENT LIABILITIES.

Bonds actually sold not less than .... £500,000 ag.
Floating debt, ... 150,000
Add various, as interest, &c., up to say May,
  1856, ... 20,000

MEANS AFFORDED BY THE LEASEES.

£30,000 per annum, covering the Bond Debt of £300,000 ag.
Four annual accruements of rent amounting
  to £10,000, the present value in Deferred
  Bonds, assumed to be 86,000
Rolling stock, &c., supposed valued 53,000

  Total future assets, ... £636,000

At least one-third of the floating debt is secured to the claimants by hypothecated bonds or other equivalents, and is consequently non-reducible.

The £30,000 per annum is required to meet in perpetuity the six per cent for annual interest upon £50,000; so that the present value of the increased rental (86,000) and the value of the rolling stock, (£50,000) forms the only fund for the defrayment of the floating debt. Hence it is certain that the creditors of the company can not receive their debts in full. About £50,000 of it being non-reducible, the creditors holding the bonds of the company as security.

It is to be hoped that there will be no holding back on the part of creditors, seeing that the present offer is likely to be the last by which they may be enabled to recover any portion of their claims against the Company. From all that we can learn, the offer of the English Company is the best that can be got. It has been accepted by the Directors of the B. B. & G. Railway Company, but the question of whether the lease will be finally ratified, remains with the creditors and shareholders to decide, by their willingness to make mutual sacrifices.

Buffalo and Pittsburgh Rail Road.

But little has been done during the past year towards completing this road, from the want of funds. Some new arrangement is about being made, so we are told, which will secure the necessary means, and we hope to see it pushed along to completion at an early day. This road is one of the absolute wants of the City, without which our prosperity will be greatly retarded, if not suspended altogether, so far as manufactures are concerned.

Buffalo is destined to become not merely a great commercial centre and depot, for she is that already, but along with and in furtherance of its commercial ascendancy, a great manufacturing City. To secure this, all we need is cheap fuel, and this can be obtained by completing the Buffalo and Pittsburgh Rail Road.

Manufactures.

It has been our custom in former annual statements to give a detailed account of the several manufacturing establishme in the city. This we omit this year, simply give the aggregate capital in the ferent branches of manufactures, and ot information of a general nature. Our son for this course this year is this. B last year and in 1853, we issued circul to the manufacturers of the city, ask them to furnish us with such informatio the amount of capital invested in their b iness, number of hands employed, valu raw material consumed, value of work tur out, where manufactures principally go, To most of these inquiries we received information which we desired, and p lished it. Parties who had given us t figures, which were probably correct, which were nevertheless below their nei bors, and were perhaps not doing half amount of business that they were, felt noyed at the contrast which appeared the several statements of, for instance, th engaged in the iron, oil and other manu turing pursuits, and invidious comparis were made and a good deal of ill feel engendered, both towards ourselves those who claimed to be doing a larger b iness than their neighbors. This year so gave us their figures quite readily, wh others were very reluctant, and some of principal ones emphatically declined, unl we would promise to use them in getting the aggregate, and not to publish th separately. For this reason we omit all tailed statements, excepting two or th where there is no competition, and wh the parties have consented that we sho use their figures.

The iron business is by far the most portant carried on in our city, and there a large number of works, which have vested a capital of over $1,250,0 Among these we might mention, as largest, the Buffalo Steam Engine Wo Shepard's Iron Works, Eagle Iron Wo Buffalo City Furnace, Vulcan Found Buffalo Iron Works, Phoenix Iron Wo Niagara Forge, Union Furnace, Eagle F nace, Clinton Iron Works. Buffalo Bolt Rivet Works and Buffalo Iron Rail Works. There are also several smaller tablishments in the city, which in the gregate turn out a large amount of wo The number of hands employed in the i iness is about 1,600, and between 8 and 10 tons of iron is annually consumed.

During the year, the Buffalo Steam Engine Works engaged in the manufacture of motives, and built two They are king preparations to extend this branch their business.

There are some twelve or thirteen Tanies located in and about the City which e employment to about 500 hands, and ich employs a capital of over $1,000,000. ere are also a number of Sheepskin Tanies in the City which dress several thoud pelts annually.

Ship building, which is probably third in ortance under the head of manufaces, as invested a capital of between $4 1,500,000, and gives employment to e 2000 hands.

There are four Agricultural Implement nufactories in operation in the City, and ourth has just been started by a new pany. The capital invested can not be than $150,000, and the number of ds employed is about 200.

There are seven establishments engaged the manufacture of Edge Tools, which the aggregate have invested a capital of ut $50,000, and give employment to ut 90 hands.

There are two extensive White Lead nufactories in the City, which employ to 45 hands, and have facilities for turnout over 1,500 tons of white lead each ar.

There are four or five Copper and Brass ndries, which have invested a capital $150,000, and which give employment some 30 men.

There are some twelve or fifteen exten- Cabinet Ware Manufactories in the y, which have invested a capital of 00,000, and employ over 600 mechanics.

There are five or six Oil Manufactories ich have invested a capital of 75 or 0,000.

We have seven or eight Piano and other sical Instrument Manufactories, giving ployment to about 425 hands, and having invested a large capital.

There are also two Shook Manufactories, en or eight Planing Mills, one Last and g Factory, four or five extensive Carriage Manufactories, two Patent Planing Mills, one extensive wholesale Boot and Shoe, one Woolen, two Rope, four Bellows, one Printing Ink, one Pail and Tub, five or six Tobacco, and one Saddlery and Coach Hardware Manufactories, besides a host of smaller, but no less important establishments, engaged in mechanical pursuits, located in the City, which turn out annually a vast amount of work, which have invested a capital of at least $7,000,000, which would make the total capital engaged in manufactures, in our City, to be not less than $12,000,000.

There is not probably a city in the Union more favorably situated than Buffalo for vending the products of industry, or as a distributing centre for those manufactures. With a surrounding county of unrivalled fertility, with the natural advantages of the extensive lake navigation and the termination of the Erie Canal—and with the several routes of transportation by railroad which radiate from her in all directions as spokes from the hub of a wheel, all that she requires to make her a great manufacturing city is an abundance of a cheap fuel. The want of natural motive power may in a great meaure be compensated for, by an abundant and cheap supply of coal. Buffalo has all the elements in possession and prospect of becoming not only a great commercial, but also an important manufacturing city.

Recapitulation.

The commercial interests of Buffalo as connected with the Lakes and canal, are the life blood of her prosperity and success, and it is therefore a matter of pride and satisfaction to all that these branches have been prosperous during the past year. The following figures show conclusively that she is entitled to the claim of being the first inland commercial city on this continent:

	Imports	Exports.
Lake	$50,346,819	$110,000,000
Canal	89,218,036	30,654,283
Central R R	35,000,000	15,000,000
Buffalo City R R	8,000,000	4,000,000
Buffalo & Erie R R	10,968,384	4,570,461
Foreign Trade	2,131,205	935,176
Total Commerce in 1855	$195,664,444	165,159,920
Total Commerce in 1854	$158,000,000	130,000,000
Increase in 1855	$37,664,444	$35,159,920

TRADE AND COMMERCE OF

Summary of Marine Disasters and Loss of Property on the Lakes for the past eight years.

	Manner of Loss	1848		1849		1850		1851		1852		1853		1854		1855	
		NO.	$ LOSS	NO.	$ LOSS	NO.	$ LOSS	NO.	$ LOSS	NO.	$ LOSS	NO.	$ LOSS	NO.	$ LOSS	NO.	$ LOSS
Steamers	Wrecked & Sunk	3	25,000	1	25,000	5	98,600	2	27,000	3	125,000	3	126,000	4	110,000	4	378,500
	Stranded	9	47,000	5	21,000	8	13,400	5	36,700	5	14,700	7	51,000	2	110,000	11	11,350
	Fire	1	20,000			5	105,000	3	35,600	2	22,000	3	156,000	2	110,000	3	44,000
	Damaged, &c	2	9,000	10	25,000	5	24,500	13	110,200	9	18,000	19	54,700	24	77,200	26	66,300
	Jettison			1	500					2	14,000			1	25,000		
	Collision			3	1,400	8	24,800	9	6,000	16	158,350	11	31,650	8	31,200	12	32,600
	Derrick														20,000		
	Total	15	101,000	20	72,900	31	265,700	32	215,500	37	352,650	43	419,350	41	463,400	56	532,750
Propellers	Wrecked & Sunk							2	55,000	4	85,000	1	42,000	5	370,000	7	351,000
	Stranded	1	12,000	1	5,000	4	2,500	6	32,800	5	6,900	7	28,900			11	9,950
	Fire	1	20,000	1	5,000	1	10,300			3	57,500			2	130,000		
	Damaged	1	1,600			1	800	5	5,000	11	38,000	10	24,500	30	63,100	34	228,150
	Jettison	1	5,000	1	3,000					4	13,200	2	2,200	7	47,000	4	13,100
	Collision	1	40			3	2,400	10	40,400	9	73,450	4	3,900	8	69,500	19	557,750
	Sunk and Raised			1	100,000												
	Total	5	39,000	4	113,000	9	16,000	23	133,200	36	274,050	24	101,500	52	680,100	75	1159,950
Barques	Wrecked & Sunk	2	18,000							2	22,000	2	19,500	3	56,000	6	116,000
	Stranded	1	1,800			2	1,100					5	4,500			6	10,800
	Fire									1	150	5	4,600	12	37,100	17	46,050
	Damaged									1	4,000					2	5,000
	Jettison									1	200			2	55,000	5	9,900
	Collision	1	600														
	Total	4	20,400			2	1,100			5	26,350	12	28,600	17	148,400	36	187,750
Brigs	Wrecked & Sunk	1	3,500	1	8,000	5	16,000	3	42,000	7	51,800	2	43,000	7	63,000	7	118,300
	Stranded	14	14,850	7	6,900	8	17,300	22	30,000	13	25,000	10	15,300			8	8,550
	Fire																
	Damaged	2	750	5	5,100	10	22,500	21	45,700	11	19,750	17	24,500	43	64,125	51	39,950
	Jettison													1	6,000	8	22,500
	Collision	2	35,800	5	4,900	4	13,100	7	16,200	6	3,350	2	2,500	6	51,000	11	26,100
	Total	19	54,900	18	24,900	27	68,900	53	133,900	38	101,100	31	85,300	55	184,125	85	215,400
Schooners	Wrecked & Sunk	19	104,800	9	46,900	15	73,600	29	89,000	21	109,300	22	111,700	41	382,626	26	182,300
	Stranded	49	54,870	23	46,000	56	64,850	62	53,250	48	70,500	48	64,300			91	161,600
	Fire				1,600			2	7,500	1	5,500	3	9,400	2	22,500	1	800
	Damaged	22	25,760	8	11,500	18	22,790	39	57,765	30	24,790	60	73,500	132	216,450	137	212,179
	Jettison			3	5,350			2	2,700	2	1,150	4	7,200	20	30,270	14	33,510
	Collision			5	13,000	7	30,500	15	34,500	18	24,950	13	21,200	9	49,150	35	97,000
	Flood at Chicago				25,000												
	Total	90	185,430	49	128,750	96	191,740	150	244,715	120	236,190	150	217,300	204	701,000	302	687,389
Scows	Wrecked & Sunk	1	1,700					2	1,700			1	1,200	2	6,000	1	2,000
	Stranded	1	1,500			3	800	2	700	1	150					4	3,700
	Fire																
	Damaged	1	900	2	1,700	2	200	2	800	3	575	2	1,100	11	3,800	6	6,900
	Jettison													1	500	1	100
	Collision													1	500	1	1,800
	Total	3	4,100	2	1,700	5	1,000	6	3,200	4	725	3	2,300	15	10,800	13	14,600
Summary	Steamboats	15	101,000	20	72,900	31	265,700	32	215,500	37	352,650	43	419,350	41	463,400	56	532,750
	Propellers	5	39,000	4	113,000	9	16,000	23	133,200	36	274,050	24	101,500	52	680,100	75	1159,950
	Barques	4	20,400			2	1,100			5	26,350	12	28,600	17	148,400	36	187,750
	Brigs	19	54,900	18	24,900	27	68,900	53	133,900	38	101,100	31	85,300	55	184,125	85	215,400
	Schooners	90	185,430	49	128,750	96	191,740	150	244,715	120	236,190	150	217,300	204	701,000	302	687,389
	Scows	3	4,100	2	1,700	5	1,000	6	3,200	4	725	3	2,300	15	10,800	13	14,600
	Flood & Derrick						25,000								20,000		
	Total	136	404,830	93	366,250	170	544,440	264	730,515	240	991,065	263	874,350	384	2187,825	567	2797,839

Aggregate of Steam and Sail Disasters, from 1848 to 1855, inclusive.

	1848	1849	1850	1851	1852	1853	1854	1855
	$ LOSS	$ LOSS	$ LOSS	$ LOSS	$ LOSS	$ LOSS	$ LOSS	$ LOSS
Steam	140,000	185,900	281,700	348,700	626,650	520,850	1,143,500	1,692,700
Sail	264,830	155,350	262,740	381,815	364,365	333,500	1,044,325	1,105,139
Total	404,830	341,250	544,440	730,515	991,015	854,350	2,187,825	2,797,839

Printed in Dunstable, United Kingdom